BUILDING with PAPER

BUILDING
with PAPER

E. Richard Churchill

Illustrated by James Michaels

Sterling Publishing Co., Inc.   New York

For Eric and Sean—two master builders

Edited by Timothy Nolan

Library of Congress Cataloging-in-Publication Data

Churchill, E. Richard (Elmer Richard)
  Building with paper / by E. Richard Churchill : illustrated by
James Michaels.
     p.   cm.
     Summary: Easy directions for building a paper town, buildings,
bridges, boats, and other projects.
     ISBN 0-8069-5772-7.—ISBN 0-8069-5773-5 (pbk.)
     1. Paper work—Juvenile literature.   [1. Paper work.
2. Handicraft.]   I. Michaels, James, ill.   II. Title.
TT870.C544   1990
745.54—dc20   89-26220
                                                        CIP
                                                        AC

1 3 5 7 9 10 8 6 4 2

Copyright © 1990 by E. Richard Churchill
Published by Sterling Publishing Co., Inc.
387 Park Avenue South, New York, N.Y. 10016
Distributed in Canada by Sterling Publishing
% Canadian Manda Group, P.O. Box 920, Station U
Toronto, Ontario, Canada M8Z 5P9
Distributed in Great Britain and Europe by Cassell PLC
Artillery House, Artillery Row, London SW1P 1RT, England
Distributed in Australia by Capricorn Ltd.
P.O. Box 665, Lane Cove, NSW 2066
Manufactured in the United States of America
All rights reserved

CONTENTS

Getting Started

In this book you will find easy and fun-to-make projects. In order to put this book to its best use, you are going to need lots and lots of stiff paper or lightweight cardboard. Notebook or typing paper will work for some of the projects but construction paper is better. The cardboard from cereal boxes or other containers is best. The cardboard tubes inside paper towel rolls and gift wrapping paper, as well as the round cardboard containers for oat cereals and salt, will also be handy. You might want to save the boxes and rolls so that you'll have them when you need them (just keep your collection neat so that your parents don't get angry). You'll also need a pair of sharp scissors, some glue, a roll of transparent tape, a ruler, and a pencil, so why not gather them up and keep them handy. Crayons, paint, soft-tip markers, and other items are going to come in handy when you decorate and design your projects.

So, now that you have everything you need, let's get started.

Let's go to work.

7

· 1 ·
Paper Town

Quick Cottage

This little house is made just by folding a sheet of paper.
Make the first one out of notebook or typing paper; then,
after you see how to construct these folded buildings, make
others using heavier paper or light cardboard.

Fold the paper in half the long way as shown in Illus. 1.
Leave the paper folded, and fold both ends along the dotted
lines as in Illus. 2.

Illus. 1

Illus. 2

It doesn't seem that Quick to me!

Quick Cottage now looks like Illus. 3. The two dotted lines show where to make the next two folds. Crease these folds well, and it will look like Illus. 4.

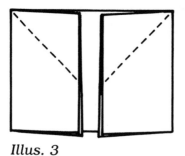

Illus. 3

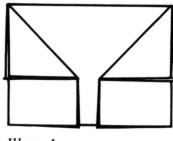

Illus. 4

Unfold the last folds so that Quick Cottage looks like Illus. 5. The dotted lines show the folds, but two of them are indicated by arrows. Reverse these two folds by folding them in the opposite direction from the way you first folded them (if they were folded back the first time, fold them forward now).

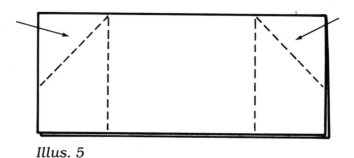

Illus. 5

Now that these two folds are flexible, it's time to form the Cottage. Hold the paper with one hand as in Illus. 6. Use one finger on the other hand to push in along the center fold as in the drawing.

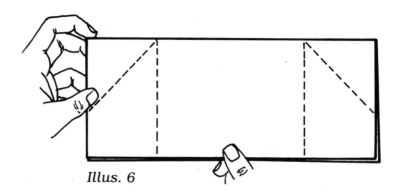

Illus. 6

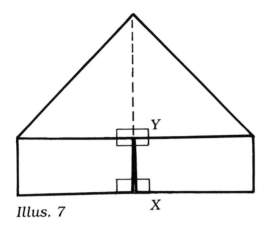

Illus. 7

X

As you push, turn the inward part so that you end up with one end of the Quick Cottage looking like Illus. 7. Put a little bit of glue or a piece of transparent tape between the sheets at the "X," then put another bit of glue or tape on the back of the end piece, at "Y." Gluing the paper together at these points will make the finished cottage stand up better. When you are finished, repeat the process for the other end of the paper, and your Quick Cottage is ready to use. It should look like Illus. 8.

Illus. 8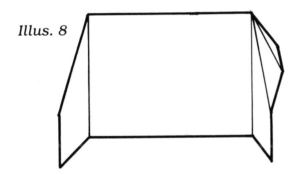

Try folding the ends flat to make it easier to color in doors and windows. An even better way is to decorate the Cottage after you have made the folds but before you glue or tape it (this will be much easier now that you know how to make the cottage).

Having made this Quick Cottage so easily, try making different-sized buildings. Just use a different-sized sheet of paper. That's all there is to it.

Try your cottage with the two folds in Illus. 8 closer to each other or nearer to the ends of the paper. This will also give the finished building a different look.

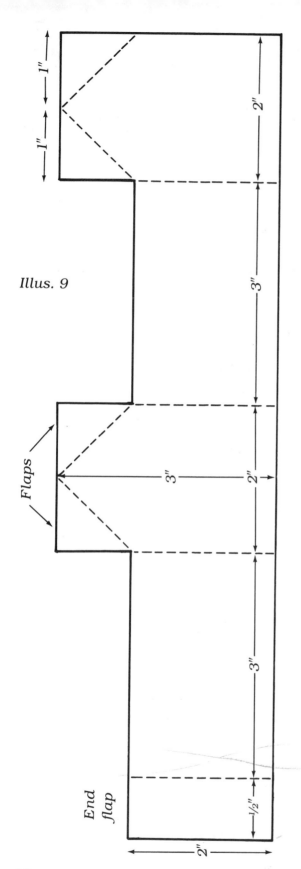

Illus. 9

Pre-Fab House

The Pre-Fab House begins with a flat piece of material. After a few folds and a little cutting, you will be able to form it into a house.

Make the first Pre-Fab House from a sheet of notebook or typing paper, since paper is easier to cut and fold than cardboard. Besides, after making this first Pre-Fab House, you can make others from notebook or construction paper.

Pre-Fab should follow the dimensions in Illus. 9. Before you begin drawing, take a good look at the drawing to see what exactly has to be done.

Two sections of the building are 3 inches wide and another two sections are 2 inches wide. Obviously, the wide sections alternate with the narrower sections, so after cutting and folding the house the two wide sections will end up opposite each other. This is very important, especially when you get ready to design Pre-Fab buildings of your own.

There's an "end flap" in Illus. 9. Make this flap wide enough to give you room to glue or tape it onto the inside of one end of the house (just don't make it wider than the end of the house!). About ½ inch or ¾ inch is about right.

Take a look at the two narrow parts of the house (it is easy to tell these are the building's ends because of the points at their tops). The point is 3 inches

14

from the base of the house, and the tip of the point is 1 inch from each side of the house's end. Don't guess at these distances—it is much better to measure them, otherwise your house may end up with its roof tipped to one side. The flaps on each side of the pointed end will fasten the Pre-Fab's roof into place, so don't cut them off.

Draw Pre-Fab according to the measurements in Illus. 9, then cut it out carefully.

When the Pre-Fab is cut out, fold it along the four lines separating the sides and ends of the house; then fold down the roof flaps. Be sure to fold them towards the inside of the house.

Now glue or tape (either one is fine) the end flap of the house in place. Make sure the flap is inside the house. If you wish, you can even staple the end flap in place. Just don't staple your finger. At this point your house looks just like Illus. 10.

Flaps

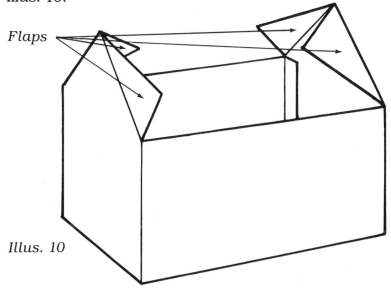

Illus. 10

CONSTRUCTION ZONE

Pre-Fab. Soon after the end of World War II a new type of house began to appear. It was called a pre-fab, which was a short form of prefabricated. A pre-fab home was built in sections at the plant, shipped in huge flat containers, then assembled on location. Almost by magic a house appeared.

Making a roof takes about thirty seconds. For this model just draw a rectangle 3 inches × 4 inches. Fold it in the middle the long way along the dotted line as in Illus. 11.

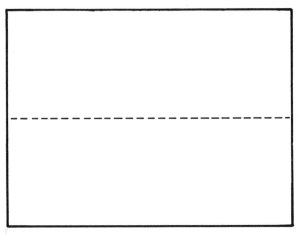

Illus. 11

To attach the roof to the house put a drop of glue on each of the four roof flaps and carefully place the roof on top of the house. With one hand inside the house and the other on the roof, press each flap onto the roof. If you are using tape, place a small piece of tape on each flap and press them onto the roof. Don't get in a hurry and the roof will not be a problem. This is one time when working with notebook paper is a bit harder than construction paper or cardboard since the thin paper may want to bend when you press the roof into place.

Every good house needs a chimney. Illus. 12 gives the dimensions for one. If you make the flap about ½ inch wide it should be perfect.

Illus. 12

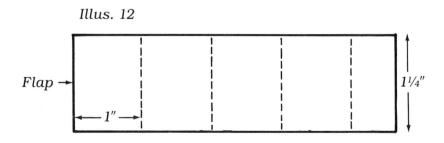

Cut the chimney out and fold it along the four corner lines; then tuck the flap inside and glue or tape the chimney together so it matches the hollow square in Illus. 13. The dotted line shows the next cut, but don't cut yet!

Hold the chimney up to one end of your Pre-Fab, as in Illus. 14.

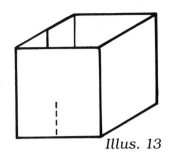

Illus. 13

See how the bottoms of the chimney sides just touch the edge of the roof? Make a little dot with your pencil or pen on the side of the chimney where the roof point touches it. It helps if you have three hands when you do this. If you are short one, maybe a friend can lend a hand.

Now cut from the bottom corner of the chimney up to the dot. Turn the chimney around and make a cut the same length on the opposite side. Be sure you make these cuts on opposite sides of the chimney.

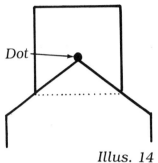

Illus. 14

The dotted lines in Illus. 15 show where to fold the base of the chimney. Fold these little triangles inside the chimney to form flaps which will help fasten the chimney to the roof. Fold in the flaps on both sides of the chimney. Now glue or tape each flap and fasten all four flaps to the roof. The finished building is as in Illus. 16.

Illus. 15

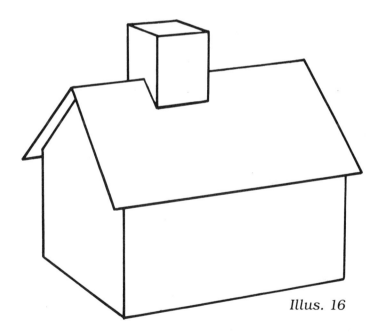

Illus. 16

This Pre-Fab House was fairly small, but to make larger buildings you just need to increase the measurements on the pattern in Illus. 9.

But what if the material you are using isn't large enough to make a big building? No problem. Just splice two pieces of material together. Lay them side by side and let one piece overlap the other by about 1 inch. Illus. 17 shows how. Run a line of glue down the overlap and in a couple of minutes you have a large piece of material ready for use. If you use tape, be sure to tape both sides of the splice.

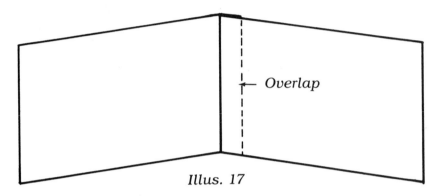

Illus. 17

If you do splice two pieces of material together, don't draw a building corner on the overlapped part of the material because the doubled-up section is difficult to fold. Make sure the overlapped section is on the side or end of the building. If you use cereal box material, plan the building so one or two of the folds in the box become corner folds for your building. When you use cereal box material, fold the building so the plain side of the box is facing out so you can color or paint doors and windows onto the sides of the building. Of course if you like the box's colors, leave the colored side out. After all, it is your building!

Super Pre-Fab

The Super Pre-Fab has a few important improvements from the Pre-Fab. Take a look at Illus. 18 before you begin drawing.

Notice that the end flap and the roof flaps are just about the same as for the Pre-Fab. However, Super Pre-Fab's roof is not going to be quite as steep as the other Pre-Fab model.

Now for the important differences. With this model building you are making the roof as a part of the basic plan. This makes it a bit easier to attach to the top of the building, but a little more difficult to measure correctly. Note the plans show

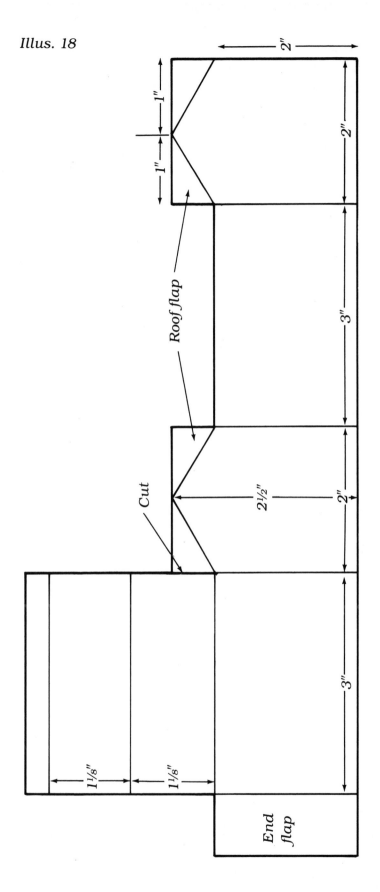

2″

1″

1″

2″

2″

Roof flap

3″

Cut

2½″

2″

1⅛″

1⅛″

3″

End flap

19

the distances along the slanted roof line at the end of the building. Measure this distance carefully; then make the two roof sections exactly as wide as the slanted edge of the roof. Since the ends of the building angle up, the slanted line is more than 1 inch long (in this case the slanted line is 1⅛ inches in length). At this point, draw the plan on a sheet of notebook paper.

Before you cut Super Pre-Fab out, take one more look at Illus. 18. See where it says "cut" in the drawing. This cut is only the height of the roof flap. If you cut all the way down that line the roof will be unmade before it is started.

Once the building is cut out, fold down the end flap and the flap at the edge of the roof; then fold down the four little triangular roof flaps. Fold the roof in the center and along the edge where it attaches to the side of the building; then fold in the building's four corners. Use a bit of glue or tape on the tabs and it becomes a building. It should look like Illus. 19.

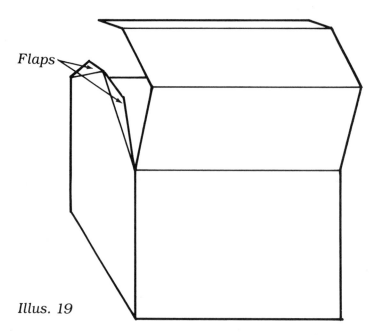

Illus. 19

Make sure the four triangular roof flaps are all folded inside the house. Put a tiny drop of glue on each one and fold the roof into place. Slip the roof flap inside the edge of the house and glue or tape it as well. Just like that your Super Pre-Fab looks like Illus.20.

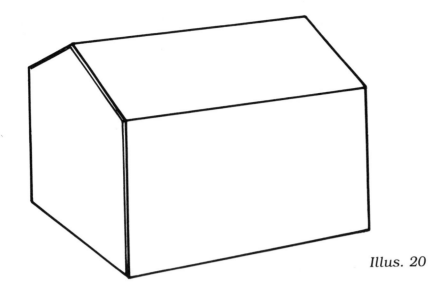

Illus. 20

Now that you see how this form of building is done, why not experiment with several other buildings of various sizes. Just remember to make the opposite sides of the buildings equal, and measure the slanted side of the roof line carefully so that the roof will fit exactly.

If you try different roofs or shapes with Super Pre-Fab, you can make all sorts of different buildings for your Paper Town. A long, thin one with a flat roof can become a small shop or a big department store, or even a row of shops all connected, as in Illus. 21. A little bit fancier building can become a restaurant as Illus. 22. Remember it's your town and your imagination so don't be afraid to try!

Though you have already figured out some ways to color or paint the finished buildings, remember that it is lots easier to color or paint them while they are still flat.

Illus. 21

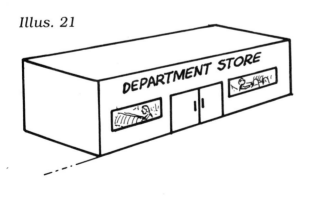

Illus. 22

Church and Steeple

Every village has a church, and making one with a tall steeple isn't very difficult.

Begin by making the church the same way you made Super Pre-Fab. Since this is a church, it should be tall and narrow. Illus. 23 gives an end view with some good measurements to use.

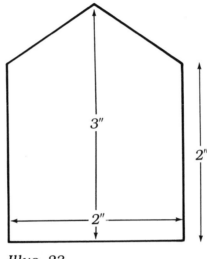

Illus. 23

How long to make the church depends upon the size of your material. If you have enough material or want to splice two pieces together, try to make your first church 6 inches long.

Making a steeple for the church isn't any problem. However, take just a minute to study Illus. 24 and read about this special type of construction before you begin cutting.

Remember to measure the distance to the center of each point of the spire. Don't guess. With the steeple it is extremely important for each point at the tip of the spire to be exactly in the center of the side. Otherwise the finished project won't look nearly as good as it should.

Look carefully at the flaps used to fasten the points of the spire together. It is necessary to cut away the material indicated with the darkened area so that the flaps don't overlap and get in the way when you fasten the points of the spire together. Since it comes to such a steep point, these flaps need to be pretty much the way they appear in the drawing.

After cutting the steeple out, fold the spire flaps down; then

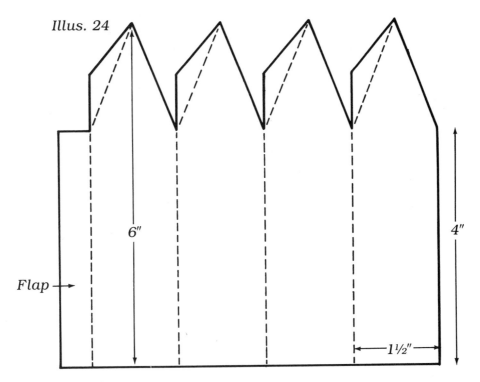

Illus. 24

fold the steeple at each corner. Tuck in the end flap and glue or tape it inside the main part of the structure.

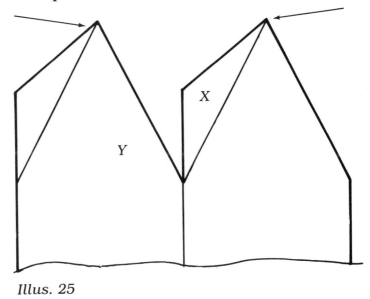

Illus. 25

Illus. 25 shows the steeple at this point. To make the spire come to a point, put a drop of glue or a piece of tape on the flap shown by the "X." Slip this flap under the "Y" section. Bend the two sections of the spire together so that their edges meet exactly. This will cause the two points shown by the arrows to come together, too.

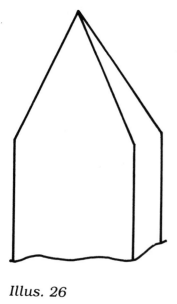

Work your way around the spire, gluing or taping each of the other flaps into place. The finished project is in Illus. 26. To fasten the steeple to the church, just use a line of glue along one side and your finished building looks like Illus. 27.

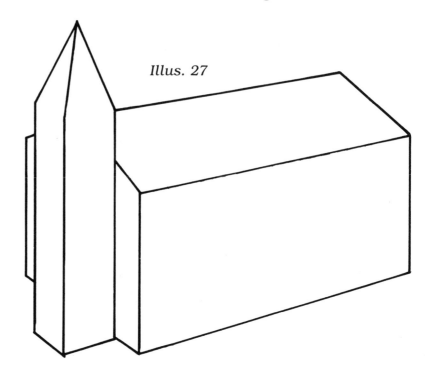

Illus. 27

Illus. 26

To give your church a fancy entrance, use the plan in Illus. 28. After cutting the entranceway out, fold the two flaps in along the dotted lines. Glue or tape them to the front of the church and it will look like Illus. 29.

Illus. 29

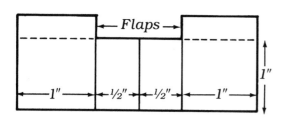

Illus. 28

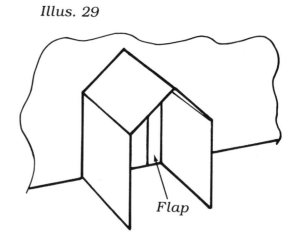

If you don't want the steeple at the side of the church, you can put a steeple on the roof instead.

Make the spire exactly the same way as the steeple except that instead of making the base 4 inches tall, try making it 2 inches high.

After the spire is finished, hold it up beside one end of the church roof. Measure it and mark it with a dot, then cut a slit up to the dot and fold the flaps back just as you did for the chimney. Do the opposite side the same way; then glue the spire onto the church. Illus. 30 shows the way this spire looks on top of the church.

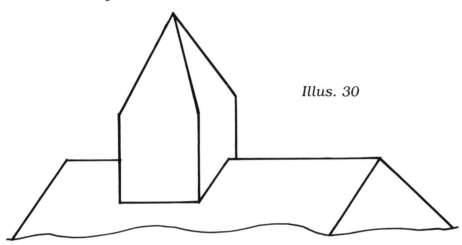

Illus. 30

Ells, Porches, and Other Ideas

To make an ell for a Pre-Fab, follow the plan shown in Illus. 31. Even though it is a bit smaller and harder to work with, you are probably skilled enough by now in making these buildings that the smaller size won't bother you.

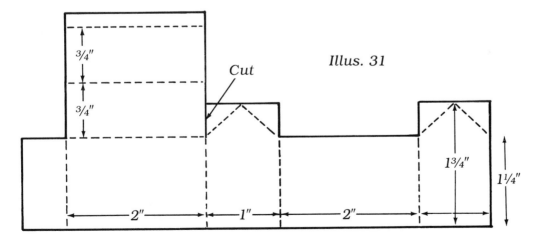

Illus. 31

Ells. Ells (not eels) are additions to buildings which extend out from the main building at right angles.

Since the end of the building is a lot narrower than the larger building, its roof is going to be steeper than in the first model even though the points of both roofs are only ½-inch higher than the tops of the other sides of the building. The steeper slant also makes the roof a little larger than you might expect. This is why you always need to measure the roof angles when you make buildings of different sizes.

After you finish your Ell, attach it to one side of the super Pre-Fab as in Illus. 32. A few drops of glue will do the job nicely.

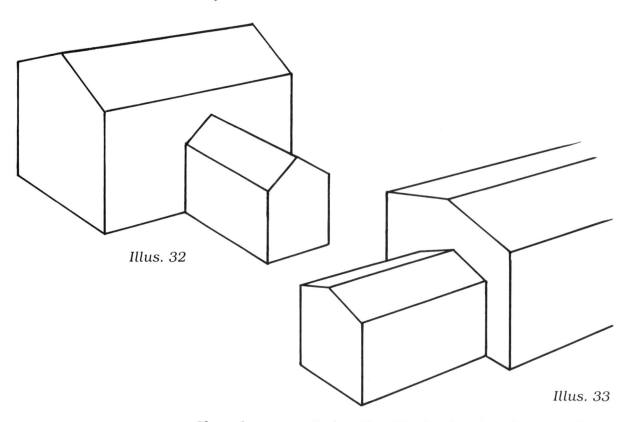

Illus. 32

Illus. 33

If you have travelled in New England or live there you have seen some of the fine old homes, especially in the country, which have additions extending out behind the main building. Illus. 33 shows this type of addition. To put them on, just take the layout from Illus. 31 and change the dimensions to what works best. Remember, though, to be careful with the roof.

How about putting a porch roof on one of your buildings? It only takes about half a minute to make one. Illus. 34 shows the plan. The cut is exactly in the center of the roof and should extend for about ⅜ inch. The two dotted lines show where to fold the flaps down after making the cut.

The dimensions in Illus. 34 will make a pretty large porch roof. Depending upon the size of other buildings you make, your porch roof can be larger or smaller.

Illus. 35 shows a porch roof in place. To fasten it to the side or end of your building, just use a bit of glue or tape on the flaps and press them firmly against the building. It's as easy as that.

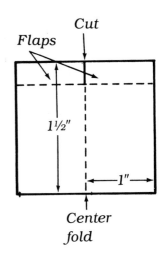

Illus. 34

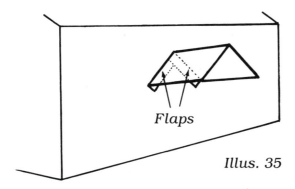

Illus. 35

Illus. 36 shows how easy it is to make a shutter. Just fold it along the dotted line and glue or tape the flap to the side of the building. Of course, windows need shutters for each side so remember to make them in pairs. Measure the window for which you wish to make shutters and then make the shutters a little taller than the window. Each shutter should be as wide from the fold to its edge as it is halfway across the window. Illus. 37 shows one pair of shutters in place beside a window.

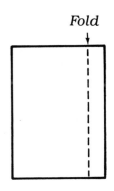

Illus. 36

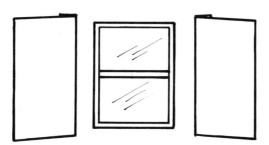

Illus. 37

If you want to have doors and windows that open, it's not very hard to make that happen. Illus. 38 shows the two cuts you need to make so a door will open and close.

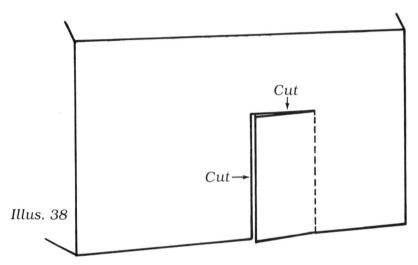

Illus. 38

Illus. 39 shows how to cut windows so they will open and close. Carefully poke the end of the scissors through the side of the building, but don't poke your fingers! Do this slowly, since it is very easy to tear the side of your building when making the first little hole.

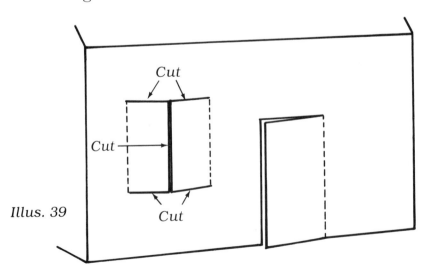

Illus. 39

You've seen huge fireplace chimneys which run up the side of a house. Making one for your buildings is really quite easy. Just make a tall, narrow, chimney like the one in Illus. 40. Since the point of the roof of our first super Pre-Fab was 2½ inches tall, make the fireplace chimney 3 inches tall.

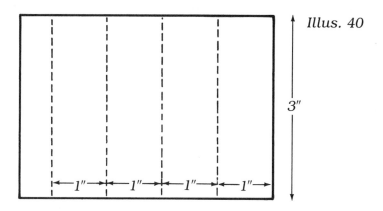

Illus. 40

3″

1″ 1″ 1″ 1″

Attach the chimney with a thin line of glue and the result looks like Illus. 41.

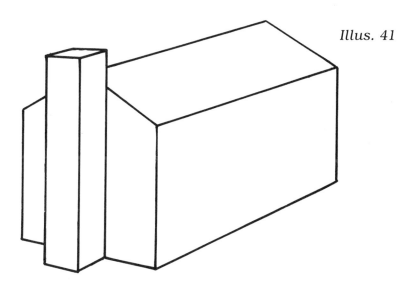

Illus. 41

CONSTRUCTION ZONE

Chimney. Chimneys are a bit taller than the house not only for good looks but also for the fire to draw properly. (In case you didn't know that, just look at the chimneys in your neighborhood.)

Quick Built

Let's look at one more way to construct a building. This one is called the Quick Built for a good reason. It is the quickest of all types of buildings to construct.

Begin with a plan like the one in Illus. 42. The dotted lines show where to make three cuts at either end of the building. Make these cuts; then fold the Quick Built building along the three lines which run from the cut at one end to the cut at the other.

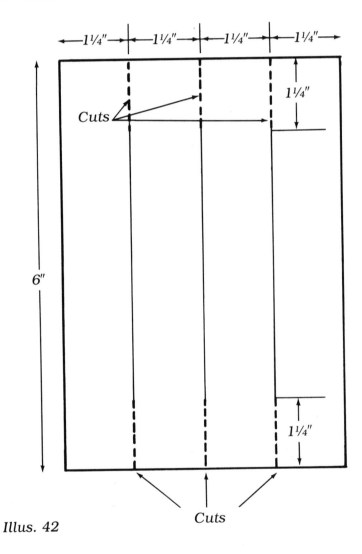

Illus. 42

To assemble Quick Built, look at the two flaps marked "X" and two marked "Y," Illus. 43. Pull the two "X" flaps together so that one overlaps the other, then pull the two "Y" flaps towards each other. Illus. 45 shows this step.

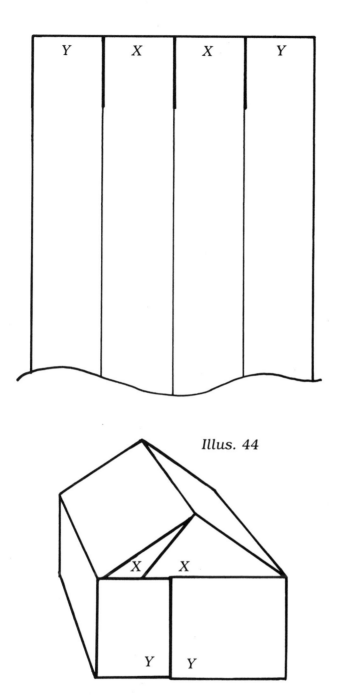

Illus. 44

By pulling the two "Y" flaps closer together Quick Built's roof gets steeper. If you move the two "Y" flaps apart a bit the roof will be not quite so steep. This could be good for stores and things like police stations.

Glue, tape, or staple the four ends flaps together when you have the roof at the angle you like; then pull the other end of the building together and fasten its flaps in place so the finished Quick Built looks like Illus. 45.

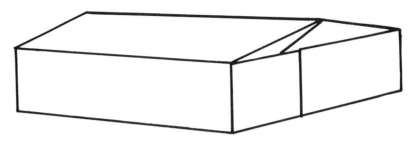

Illus. 45

Make Quick Built buildings wider by changing the measurements for the two center sections and by making the end flaps longer than the ones in the model we just built. Illus. 46 shows this. It also shows how to lengthen the end flaps so they will still overlap as you widen the building.

Illus. 46

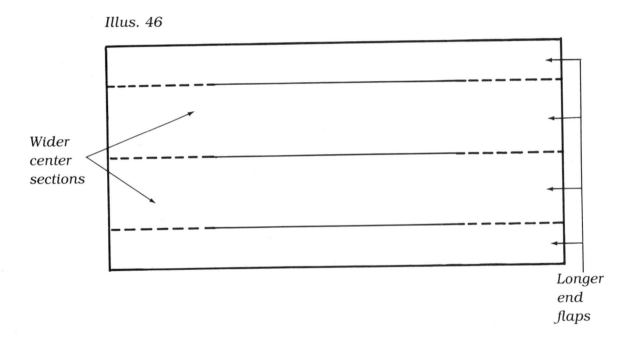

Wider center sections

Longer end flaps

These buildings are good for large stores, small houses and garages, even dog houses. Though you will probably want to use cereal box cardboard or manila folder material, there is nothing wrong with building a village using notebook or typing paper. The size buildings you decide on will depend upon the size of any cars and trucks you may wish to use with the finished village.

That's a little too quick.

City Hall

Every community needs a city hall to be the center of government. How large or how small the city hall is depends a lot upon the size of your village or town. For that matter the sort of building used for your city hall will depend upon the size of the village you are building.

Choose a type of building for city hall. Make it larger than the houses and other buildings in town so it is easy to spot among the other buildings.

Most city halls have an ell or two to make them larger and more impressive. Illus. 47 shows one possible city hall design.

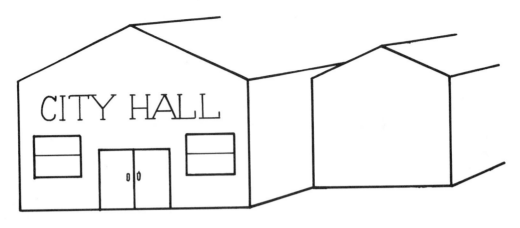

Illus. 47

Large buildings often have flat roofs. If you are planning to enlarge your village into a town or city think about a city hall with a flat roof.

Illus. 48 shows one way to construct a building with a flat roof. You can make your city hall larger or smaller than the one shown, of course.

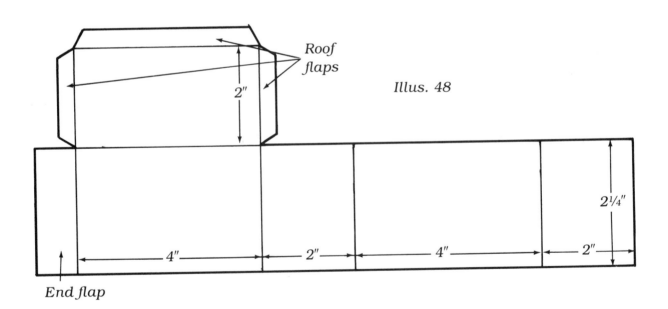

Roof flaps

Illus. 48

2"

2¼"

4"

2"

4"

2"

End flap

Glue or tape the end flap into place first; then, after creasing the roof flaps down, tuck them inside the building. Fasten them firmly into place with glue or tape and just like that you have built a city hall with a flat roof.

Remember that it is lots easier to draw or paint on a building when it is flat, so draw in windows and letter CITY HALL on the front of the building before you assemble it.

To give City Hall or any building a little variety, draw in bricks or stonework for its walls. Again, be sure to do this before putting the building together. Illus. 49 shows several types of brick or stone walls to draw onto the sides of the City Hall or any other building you make.

Illus. 49

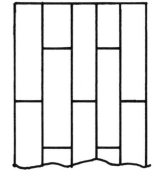

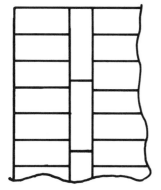

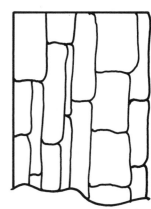

Schools

Every village or town needs at least one school. A small village may very well have a school building with a peaked roof just like some of the homes we made earlier. A larger town or city will probably have more than one school, and they will have flat roofs, just like the city hall.

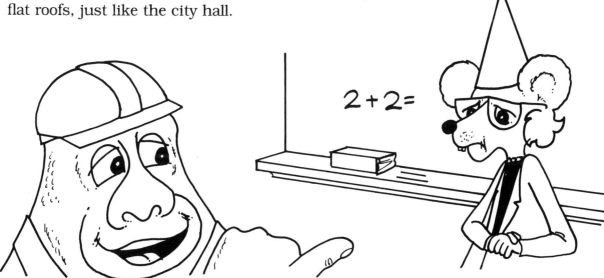

2 + 2 =

Schools are often only one storey high but quite long and wide. This means you may need to splice the material you are using to build your village. Remember that when you splice or join two pieces of material it is usually best to overlap them ½ inch or so, then use tape or glue to fasten the two pieces together.

Here's a hint when working with schools or any large building. Plan your building so one end of the splice where you joined two pieces of material comes at a corner. By folding the paper or cardboard at one side of the splice you avoid having the double thickness come in the middle of a wall where it is easier to see. Illus. 50 shows a splice and where to place the corner so the fold comes right at the edge of the double layer of material.

Illus. 50

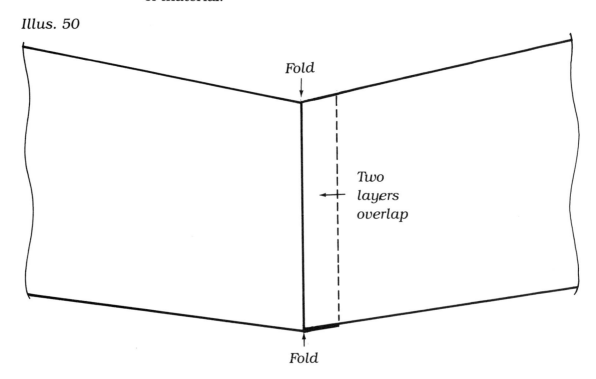

Fold

Two layers overlap

Fold

Schools usually have more windows than do homes or city halls and other buildings. Keep this in mind when you do the art work on your school building.

Many schools have several wings. Make each section separately; then glue or tape the wings together just as you did the ells in some of the buildings you have already built. Illus. 51 shows an overhead view of a school building with two wings.

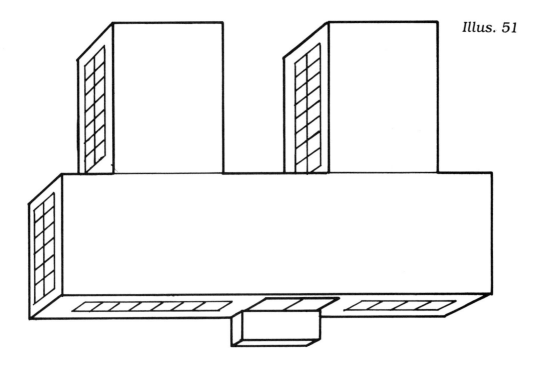

Taller Buildings and Skyscrapers

By now your original town has grown into a small city, so there is no reason for your growing community not to have at least one skyscraper.

Unless you have a supply of very large sheets of construction paper or lightweight cardboard you will have to splice several sheets together to build taller buildings.

To disguise the point at which two sheets of material are joined together, plan to draw or paint a ledge or a series of windows along the splice. This will hide the seam after the two pieces of material are taped or glued together. If your building does not work out so you can have a ledge at the splice, don't worry about it.

A skyscraper is really just a tall, thin Super Pre-Fab. Keep in mind that buildings look taller when they are slim and narrow. However, these buildings are easily tipped or blown over. Be sure your skyscrapers and tall buildings are wide enough so they aren't in any danger of falling over.

Skyscrapers may have flat roofs or pointed ones. Most sky-scrapers have several sections. Join some ells to the main building to make skyscrapers which have sections of different heights and shapes. Illus. 52 shows several ways you can join sections together to construct interesting skyscrapers.

There is no limit to the number, size, or type of buildings you can make. How much your village grows, or how much art work is on each building, depends completely on you. You're the city planner.

This is a great project for you and your friends to work on together. You can stop at any time and play with your buildings, or keep adding new buildings as long as you wish to expand your community.

CONSTRUCTION ZONE

Skyscraper. Skyscraper is a name given to any tall building. The first skyscrapers were built in Chicago and New York. This was because land was so costly it was necessary to build as many floors as possible on one building site.

Iron girders which made the frame or skeleton of skyscrapers made it possible to construct buildings with many floors. Today the iron has been replaced by steel and concrete.

Oh, you beast!

· 2 ·
Bridges

Pier Bridge

The pier bridge was one of the earliest types of bridges built, so it will be the first bridge we build. Make three supports (or piers) first. Use cereal box material or any fairly heavy paper. Notebook or typing paper is good, too, but it won't be as strong.

Illus. 53 shows you the dimensions for the piers.

To assemble the pier, fold it along each of the dotted lines shown in the drawing. Form it into a rectangle 1 × 3 inches and tuck the end flap under. Glue or tape the end flap to the opposite end so that the pier looks just like a little house. Now, crease the top flaps down and fold the top into place. Tuck the flaps inside the pier and glue or tape them into place. Make two more piers just like the one already made.

Modern piers are made with concrete but older ones were constructed of rock or brick. So, you want to draw or paint the rocks before you fold the pier into place.

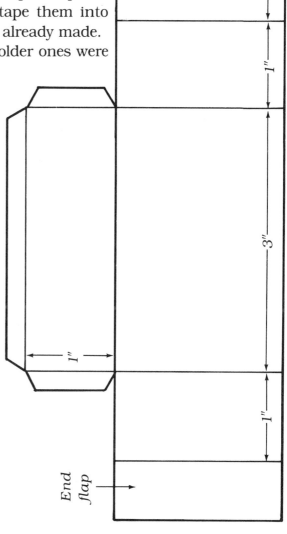

Illus. 53

CONSTRUCTION ZONE

Mortar. Mortar is a mixture of cement, lime, sand, and water that is used to hold rocks or bricks together.

Arch. An arch is a curve with the rounded part pointing upwards. It is used to cross an open area and hold up a bridge or part of a building.

Keystone. The keystone is wider at the top than at the bottom. It fits into the highest point at the center of an arch. Both sides of the arch push against the keystone which keeps the arch from falling.

CONSTRUCTION ZONE

Building Bridges. Since people began to travel they have needed to cross rivers, canyons and other natural barriers. The first bridges were logs which were dragged into place over narrow places in streams and rivers. Then came rocks piled in the middle of wider rivers to allow people to walk along from log to the rocks; then to the other log and so on until they crossed the river. Later, when wider bridges were needed, people joined the logs together side by side. Later on, planks were cut from logs to make better bridges with smooth surfaces.

Stone bridges soon followed. Chunks of flat stones were laid from one pile to another just as logs were first used for foot bridges. Soon came stones cemented together to make a more lasting bridge.

The Romans discovered the arch. Once a keystone was in place at the top of the arch's curve, a bridge could hold up great weights. Steel arches are still used today.

When iron and steel came into use it was possible to construct bridges thousands of feet long. Today's builders use concrete and steel to build bridges our ancestors would not have thought possible.

For the bridge itself, a piece of paper or cereal box material 11 or 12 inches long and 6 inches wide is perfect. Fold the long sides up along the dotted lines shown in Illus. 54. Crease them sharply so the sides stand up.

Illus. 54

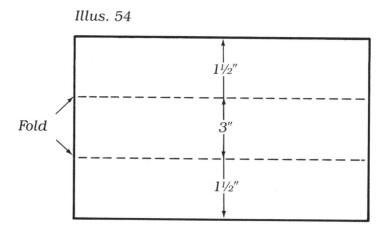

Fold both sides down along the dotted lines as in Illus. 55. Fold the upper edge towards the outside of the bridge and crease the material well along this fold. A bit of glue or tape may help here.

Illus. 55

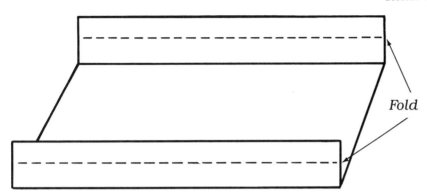

Fold

All that is left is to set the three piers up so that one is at each end of the bridge and the third pier is in the middle to keep the bridge from sagging.

There is no limit as to how long or how high you can build a pier bridge. Famous old London Bridge was a pier bridge made pretty much like this one.

To build a long pier bridge, just splice sections of bridge together. Overlap the ends of the sections about ½ inch and glue or tape them together. Make enough piers to hold up the longer bridge.

Bridge builders found it was possible to make a long pier bridge higher in the center than at either end. This gave it a bit more strength and made it look better. To do this make the middle piers a bit taller than the ones at the end. Don't raise the center of the bridge too much or you will end up with a crooked bridge.

CONSTRUCTION ZONE

Pier. A pier is a support in the bed of a river or low spot to hold the middle of a bridge.

Causeway. Very long pier bridges that cross swamps or wet areas are called causeways. A causeway is a raised road or highway across wet ground or water.

Illus. 56

Truss Bridge

It isn't always possible to build piers to hold up the middle of a bridge, especially if it is needed over a deep canyon. That's where the truss bridge comes in.

Begin with a bridge the size of our first pier bridge. Use a piece of paper or cereal box material 11 × 6 inches. Glance back at Illus. 54 on page 44 for the bridge surface.

Cut four pieces of cereal box material 7 inches long and about ⅝ inch in width. These are the trusses. Very carefully make holes in each end of each of the four pieces. Illus. 56 shows where. A small paper punch is great for this hole punching, but you could also use the point of a ballpoint pen, a compass point, or an awl. Just don't punch holes in your finger or in the top of a table! A good idea is to place a pad of newspaper under any material you are poking.

Now punch three holes on each side of the bridge itself. Illus. 51 shows where these holes should be. Make certain the center hole is exactly halfway between the two end holes.

Illus. 57

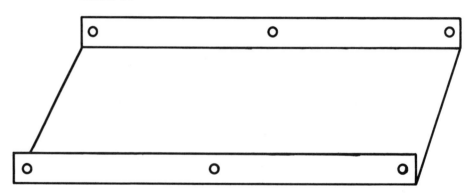

Illus. 58

Take two pieces of cereal box material, each 4 inches long and about ⅝-inch wide. These are going to become the bridge's tie rods. Make a hole in each end of each tie rod. To make your truss bridge look a bit more professional, round off the ends of the trusses and tie rods as in Illus. 58. You don't have to do this but it adds a bit of class to your bridge.

Paper fasteners are a great help with constructing the bridge, but small paper clips will also do the job just fine.

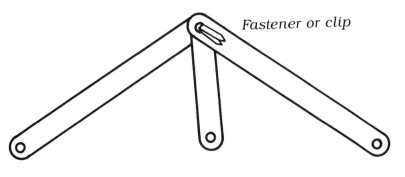

Fastener or clip

Illus. 59

Connect two trusses and one tie rod with a paper fastener or paper clip as in Illus. 59. If you are using paper clips you'll probably have to open one end of the clip out a bit before connecting the two trusses and tie rod. Be sure to bend the clip back into place once it is in place.

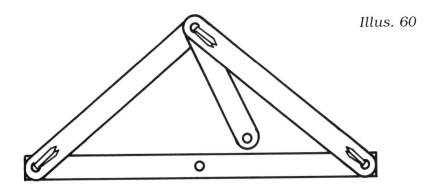

Illus. 60

Join the other ends of the trusses to the holes at either end of the bridge, so the truss bridge looks like Illus. 60. Fasten the loose end of the tie rod to the hole in the center of the bridge and one side of your truss bridge is complete. It looks like Illus. 61.

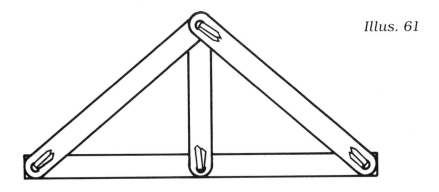

Illus. 61

Build the other side of the bridge in the same way and the truss bridge is ready for use.

If the bridge needs to be a bit stronger, put a brace in place between the tops of the tie rods on either side of the bridge. Cut a piece of cereal box material 1 inch longer than the width of the bridge. It should be about ⅝-inch wide.

Fold each end up ½ inch as in Illus. 62.

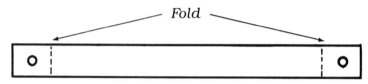

Illus. 62

Make a hole in each end as seen in the drawing. Loosen the paper fastener or paper clip which holds the two trusses and tie rod and add this cross brace. Refasten the clip with the brace attached. Do the same for the other side of the bridge and the cross brace is in place.

CONSTRUCTION ZONE

Trusses. Trusses are planks fastened together so all of them help support the weight of the bridge.

Building Tips. Bridge builders found out hundreds of years ago that triangles would not collapse. That's why the trusses and tie rods form triangles.

Tough Truss

For a more complicated truss bridge, begin with a bridge surface about 25 inches long. Join two pieces of material together if necessary. Next, cut two pieces of cereal box material, each 19 inches long and ¾-inch wide. These are the big trusses for your bridge.

Illus. 63 shows how to locate the holes in the trusses and the bridge itself.

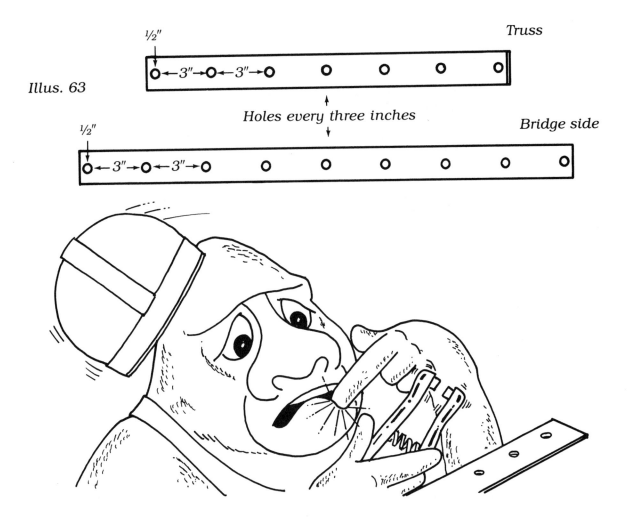

Illus. 63

½″   Truss

←3″→ ←3″→

Holes every three inches

½″   Bridge side

←3″→ ←3″→

Make fourteen tie rods; seven for each side of the bridge. Cut these about ⅝-inch wide and about 4½ inches long. Make the holes in each end of the tie rod, making certain they are exactly 4 inches apart. This leaves about a ¼ inch of the tie rod beyond the center of the hole. Make the tie rods a bit longer if you are having trouble making the hole without hurting the end of the tie rod.

Cut sixteen beams each 5½ inches long and about ⅝-inch wide. Make a hole in each end just as with the tie rods, and make them 5 inches apart. Use the paper fasteners or paper clips to put the tie rods and trusses together.

It is a good idea to make three or four horizontal braces to join the trusses on one side of the bridge with those on the other. It is also a good idea to install these braces as you attach the tie rods to the trusses.

This bridge is pretty complicated because of all those 5-inch diagonal braces to install as well as the tie rods. Check Illus. 64 for help. It shows the bridge-building step by step. If you forget to put in a brace just go back, loosen the paper fastener or paper clip, and slip the brace into place. Don't get in a hurry and remember to add a diagonal brace each time you add a tie rod.

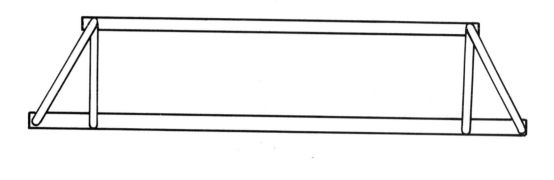

Illus. 64

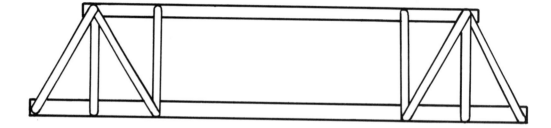

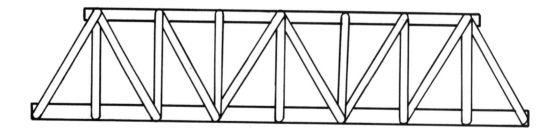

Once you have all the tie rods and diagonal braces in place, as well as three or four horizontal braces, your bridge is complete.

Suspension Bridge

Build the suspension bridge about 2 feet long. Go ahead and make the road surface first, just as in the Truss Bridge (page 46). At both ends of the bridge surface make two holes, as in Illus. 65.

Illus. 65

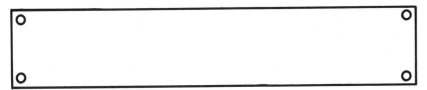

I can suspend a bridge!   *I don't think that's what they meant.*

CONSTRUCTION ZONE

Suspension Bridge. Suspension bridges have been around for only about the last two hundred years. The earliest suspension bridges used ropes to hold the bridge platform up. Modern suspension bridges use wires and cables to support the bridge.

Though suspension bridges can be quite attractive—for years tourists have visited the famous Golden Gate suspension bridge and willingly paid a toll fee to be able to say they drove across it—they have one major fault. They tend to sway or swing in the wind or with lots of weight on them. Major suspension bridges are so strong there is seldom any need to worry, but small suspension bridges used for foot traffic can be quite exciting if they begin to shake and sway.

The suspension bridge needs two piers, one to support either end. Look back at Illus. 55 (page 43) to see how to make these piers. Adjust the measurements so the piers will be as wide as the base of the bridge. For this first bridge let's build piers which are 2 inches high.

Now to make the towers which support the bridge. Cut out four pieces of material, each about 12 inches long and 7 inches wide. Illus. 66 shows how to fold each piece of material to form a hollow tower 12 inches high and 1½ inches across. After creasing each fold, tuck the end flap in and either glue or tape it in place.

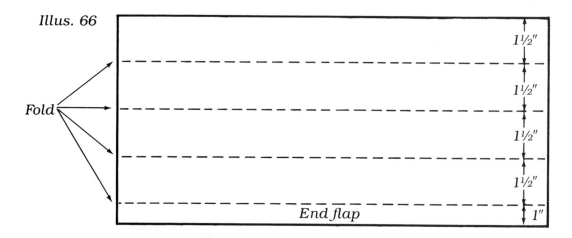

Illus. 66

Fold

1½"
1½"
1½"
1½"
1"

End flap

To assemble the towers, take two of these hollow pieces and place them side by side, and measure the bridge surface you made to begin this bridge.

Draw a section on a piece of cereal box material that is exactly 2 inches high (because the piers are 2 inches high). Make this drawing as wide as the bridge plus 3 inches, 1½ inches for each tower. Cut four pieces of cereal box material to this plan, shown in Illus. 67.

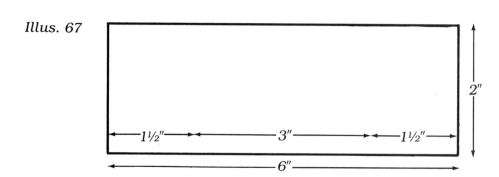

Illus. 67

1½" — 3" — 1½"
2"
6"

Glue or tape one of the pieces you just made to the base of the two towers you placed side by side. Be sure to space the towers just far enough apart so the bridge base will fit between them. Illus. 68 shows the construction thus far. Now turn this construction over and glue or tape a second piece of material to the other side. The two tower pieces can count as one tower. Make the second tower the same way.

Very carefully cut a notch about ½-inch deep in the tops of each tower, as in Illus. 69. These will hold the main cables in place. Cut this cable notch in both sides of each hollow tower column.

Illus. 68

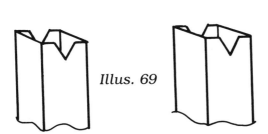

Illus. 69

It is now cable time. Take two pieces of heavy string or cord for the main cables. Each piece has to be long enough to extend from the hole in one end of the bridge base, up to the first tower, over the tower to the second tower, and down to tie into the hole at the other end of the bridge.

Illus. 70

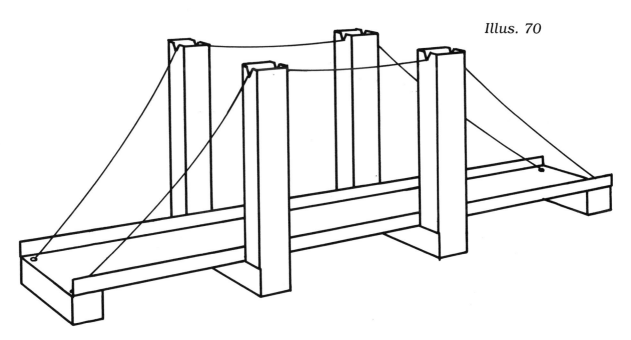

Illus. 71

Tie one end of the cable first; then string the cable before cutting the string or cord. Illus. 70 shows how to leave some slack in the cable to give your suspension bridge a nice look and allow you to attach the wires (thread or string) which support the base of the bridge. Just make certain both cables have exactly the same amount of slack in them.

Use thread or thin string to attach the cables to the bridge. Carefully poke a hole in the side of the bridge: don't poke your finger! A pin is good to use if you are using thread. Tie an end of the thread through the hole and tie the other end to the cable. Do the same for the opposite side of the bridge and make certain the threads across from each other are exactly the same length. Illus. 71 shows this.

How many wire threads you use is up to you. The more you use the more realistic your suspension bridge appears.

If you have trouble making the holes in the side of the bridge surface, here's a hint. Decide how many wires you want; then remove the bridge from the towers and lay it on one side on a thick newspaper. Make the holes in one side of the bridge, then turn it over. Just make certain the holes on one side are exactly across from those on the other.

Make longer suspension bridges with three or four towers if you wish (and if you have what it takes to tie all those wires into place).

CONSTRUCTION ZONE

Cables. The cables used in suspension bridges are made of hundreds or even thousands of smaller wires which are bound together. The largest suspension bridge cables are as much as 3 feet across.

Bridge building. Marching soldiers do not ever cross a small suspension bridge marching in step. If they do, their weight shifting at the same time will cause a small suspension bridge to sway dangerously.

Drawbridge

Perhaps the best-known drawbridge in the world is London's Tower Bridge, so our drawbridge will be similar to Tower Bridge (why not go with the best!).

London Bridge is falling down.

First, make the two towers. Make them at least 12 inches high and 4 inches across, so take a sheet of cereal-box material 12 × 17 inches (four sides each, 4 inches wide, plus 1 inch for the end flap equals 17 inches.)

Glance back at Illus. 66 on page 52 in case you don't remember how to fold the material to make a tower. Make folds every 4 inches.

After folding the material, but before gluing or taping it into a tower, make the cuts in Illus. 72. These should be about 2 inches from the bottom of the material. Make the cuts about ⅛-inch wide. If you want to give your towers the "London" look, cut out two small sections from each side, as in Illus. 73. With these done, glue or tape the material into a tower shape.

Illus. 72

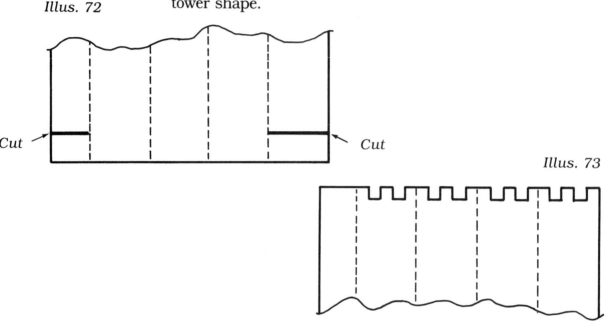

Cut →   ← *Cut*

Illus. 73

Cut two pieces of material, each 11 or 12 inches long and 3½ inches wide. These will form the bridge itself.

Fold one end of each piece and crease it sharply as in Illus. 74. This fold should be ½ inch from the end of the material. After making the fold, carefully punch two holes near the opposite end of the bridge. These holes are also in Illus. 74.

Illus. 74

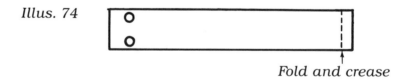

Fold and crease

To begin building, slip the folded end of the bridge through the slit in the tower, so the folded end sticks down towards the bottom of the tower. Otherwise, when you raise the drawbridge it is likely to slip out of the base of the tower.

Once the bridge is in place, lift it up so it is nearly against the tower. Illus. 75 shows how. Mark the front of the tower with two dots just a bit higher than the two holes you punched in the bridge.

Now lower the bridge. Very carefully make two holes in the front of the tower at these two dots; then make two more holes in the rear of the tower so they are exactly across from and in line with the holes in the front.

It's time to hook up the bridge. Cut two pieces of string long enough to reach from the bridge in the lower position up to the tower and then through the tower. Illus. 76 shows one string in place.

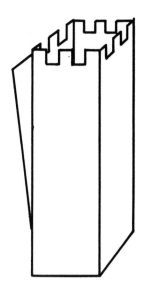

Illus. 75

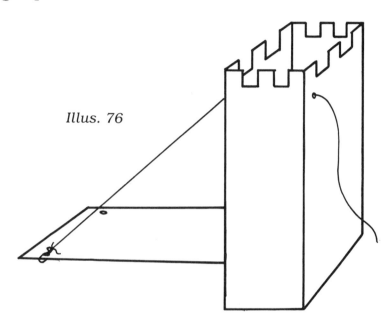

Illus. 76

Tie the string to the bridge, and then run the loose end through the front of the tower. Reach inside the tower for the string's end and push it on through the back of the tower. Do the same for the other side of the bridge, and when the two strings are both through the rear of the tower, tie them together.

To raise the drawbridge pull the string slowly back and watch the bridge come up.

Build the second tower and bridge in the same way and you now have a double drawbridge just like famous Tower Bridge in London.

Try designing and building other drawbridges if you wish. Not all drawbridges are double bridges like Tower Bridge. A smaller drawbridge with only one lifting side is just the thing to cross a small river or stream.

· 3 ·
Boats

For your first boats, it is a good idea to use notebook, and typing or computer paper. Once you have made some paper boats, try using cereal box material. Just remember to work slowly with cereal box material and make sure to crease the folds well.

What do you know about boats?

They float!

CONSTRUCTION ZONE

Bow. The bow of a boat or ship is its front and the stern is found at the rear or back of the craft.

Amidships. Amidships is halfway between the bow and stern.

Ship. Any boat or ship may be called a craft but large crafts are called ships. Boats are smaller.

Thwart. The seat in a small boat is a thwart.

Port. Port is to the left of a boat or ship.

Starboard. Starboard is to its right.

Hawser. A hawser is the heavy rope used to connect barges.

Pram

A pram is a flat-bottomed rowing boat with square or blunt bow and stern. Illus. 77 shows the plan for the pram. As you can see, it is just a little wider amidships than at the bow or stern.

Illus. 77

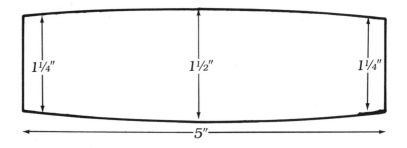

Here's a hint to make the pram exactly the same on its port side as the starboard side. Fold the paper in half; then draw half the plan. Illus. 78 shows this step (remember the fold in your paper goes along the bottom of the drawing).

Illus. 78

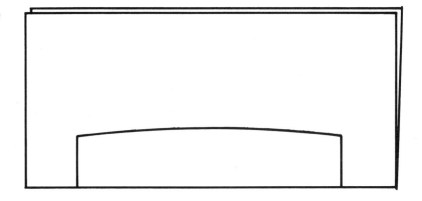

Cut out the plan and unfold it. Draw around it on a second sheet of paper. Leave about 2 inches of cutting room on all sides of the drawing.

Now enlarge the plan by 1 inch in all directions. One way to do this is shown in Illus. 79. Another method is to fold your plan and slip it over another folded sheet of paper; then draw around it as in Illus. 80. Either method works. If you use the folded method, cut out the second drawing and trace it on the boat-building paper. Just make sure you line your new plan up correctly so you don't end up with a lopsided pram.

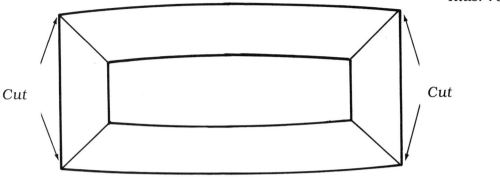

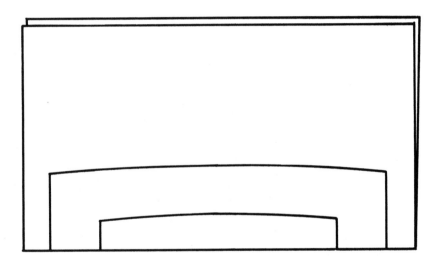

Cut out the pram, cutting only around the larger drawing. Make the four cuts shown in Illus. 79.

To assemble your pram, place the paper flat on the table before you. With your thumbs on the inside of the boat, use your fingers to bend the sides upwards, one at a time. As you do this the sides will bend outward, giving the pram a gentle curve on either side.

If this does not happen, stop and retrace the lines inside the pram. A ballpoint pen is good for this. It makes a little crease in the paper, and it would be just enough to cause the paper to follow the line as you gently fold the sides of the craft upwards.

Now fold the bow and stern up into place. This is easy because these folds are straight lines. Illus. 81 shows things at this point.

Illus. 81

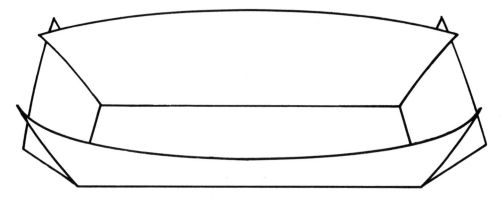

To finish your pram, tuck the ends of both sides inside the stern and glue or tape them in place. Fold or trim the loose ends of the stern around the sides and glue or tape again. Repeat the process for the bow and your pram is ready to have a couple of thwarts put in place.

A strip of paper ¾-inch wide is perfect for a thwart. Measure the distance from one side of the pram to the other and cut the thwart ½ inch or so longer than that distance.

Fold down each end of the thwart about ¼ inch and slip the seat into place. Glue or tape the folded ends to the side of the pram and the thwart is in place. Do the same for a second thwart and the finished pram looks pretty much like Illus. 82.

Illus. 82

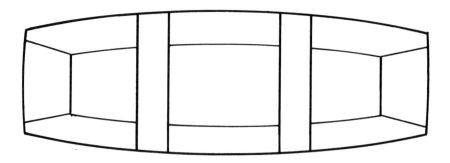

Try making prams larger or smaller, or use the same construction method and build rowboats which have wider sterns and much narrower, more pointed bows. Illus. 83 shows some ideas. Here's a hint, however. The more pointed the bow is, the harder it is to make the paper behave when you try to shape the boat's curved sides.

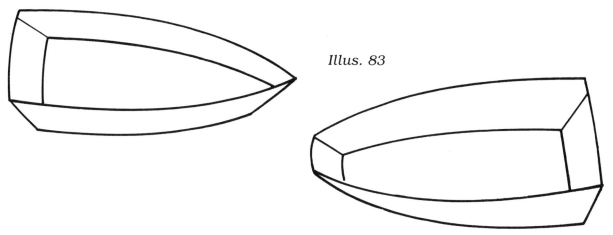

Illus. 83

Experiment with rowboats whose sterns are wider than those of a pram and whose bows are narrower. Go slowly and don't try to make a boat with a pointed bow the first time.

Remember, if you decide to make prams and rowboats which are larger than our first pram, make the sides a bit higher than 1 inch. The higher sides and stern are needed to go with the larger boat.

Tugs and Barges

For your first barge you need a piece of stiff paper or cereal box cardboard 6 × 11 inches.

CONSTRUCTION ZONE

Hatch. A hatch is an opening in the deck which allows people or goods to go below deck.

Aft. Aft means towards the rear or stern.

Forward. Forward is towards the front or bow of a craft.

Barges. Barges are the working cargo carriers of many major rivers. These flat-bottomed craft haul everything from coal to garbage as they move slowly along the waterways.

Draw the barge bottom as in Illus. 84. The reason the ends are 1½ inches long while the sides are only 1 inch in height is because the sides on this barge are vertical. The bow and stern are both slanting, which requires them to be a bit longer.

Illus. 84

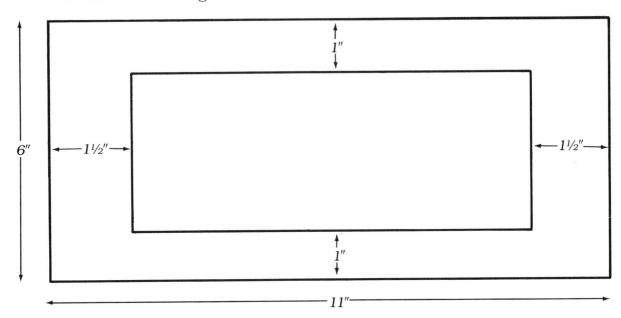

The next drawing, Illus. 85, shows four solid lines. These are the four cuts necessary to get the barge started. Make these four cuts; then fold the ends of the bow and stern upwards along the dotted lines in the drawing.

Illus. 85

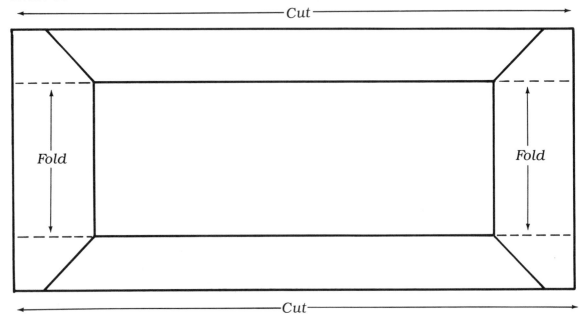

Now flatten the material out. Since the bow and stern on this barge look exactly the same, start with one end or the other and call it the bow. Fold the bow up along the line from Illus. 85 and crease the fold. Do the same for the stern. Flatten the bow and stern down and fold both sides of the barge up and crease them.

Pull the bow up so that its folded ends are outside the barge's sides. Glue or tape the folded ends into place. The ends of the stern will stick up above the barge sides as seen in Illus. 86. Fold the tip of each end over so it is now inside the barge. Glue or tape it down. Assemble the stern in the same way and your barge is almost ready for action.

Illus. 86   *Fold over*

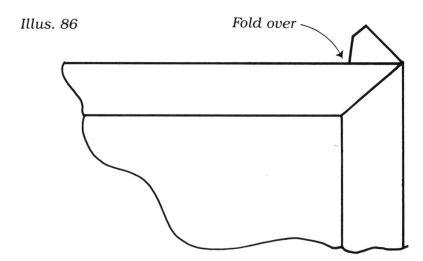

Since barges have no power of their own they are pulled or pushed by tugboats. Often a tug can pull as many as half a dozen or more barges.

In order to pull barges or connect them together there has to be something for the hawsers to attach to.

Cut a piece of notebook paper about 1½ × 1½ inches. Roll it tightly and tape or glue the loose end. Tape or glue the roll to the side of the barge as in Illus. 87. Repeat this step so all four corners of the barge are equipped for the hawsers. Your hawsers can be any kind of twine you find around the house.

Illus. 87

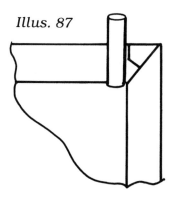

Make as many barges as you need for your fleet. They may be larger or smaller than the one you just made—it is up to you.

But the toot, toot, toot doesn't mean a hoot . . .

Barges need a tugboat to work, so begin the tug by designing the bottom of the hull. Once again the best way to make certain of having a hull which is the same on both sides is to draw a plan using folded paper.

Illus. 88 shows the folded plan for the bottom of the tug-

Illus. 88

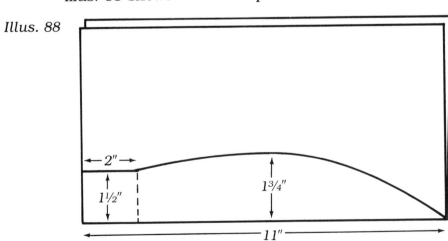

2"

$1\frac{1}{2}$"

$1\frac{3}{4}$"

11"

68

boat's hull. Try to come fairly close to the drawing but don't worry if it's not perfect. After making one tugboat this way you can change the design any way you wish.

Cut out the plan and unfold it. Trace the plan onto cereal box material and cut it out. Fold the stern section up along the dotted line as in Illus. 88. Crease it so the stern stands upright.

Now place the bottom of the hull on another piece of cereal box material and trace around it to form the piece shown in Illus. 89, only don't include the upright stern in your drawing.

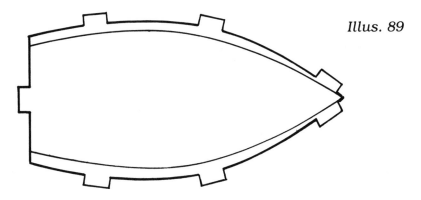

Illus. 89

Before starting to draw, note several things about Illus. 89. Trace the stern and bow exactly, but, as you trace around the port and starboard sides, make the second piece anywhere from ⅛ to ¼ inch wider than the bottom of the hull; then add three tabs on either side of the pattern, and one tab at the stern.

When you have traced this second piece, just put it to one side for the moment. Eventually it is going to become the deck of your tugboat.

It's the chugga, chugga, chugga that makes it go!

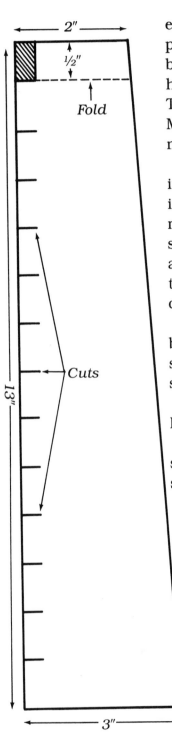

Illus. 90

2"

½"

Fold

13"

Cuts

3"

The next things to make are the sides of your tug. Illus. 90 shows a design for the sides of the hull. You can use cereal box material if you wish but fairly stiff paper will work just as well.

The sides are lower at one end than the other. The lower end is going to be at the stern of your tug. Keep the bottom part of the sides straight. The part that rises from stern to bow is the top. The sides are longer than the bottom of the hull because they have to form around the curve in the hull. They are also going to fold around the stern and the bow. Making them a bit longer than necessary is okay—just don't make them too short!

Cut out the corner of material at the stern (the shaded area in Illus. 90); then make the cuts along the bottom edge every inch or so. These cuts should be about ⅜-inch long. Try to make every cut exactly the same as others. If you are using stiff paper, draw just one side and cut out two layers of paper at once. Otherwise, draw one side and use it as a pattern for the second side. Once the sides are cut out and all those little cuts are made, it's time to begin building the tug.

If you plan to paint the tug, you can wait until the tug is built. However, if you are using crayons, you need to color the sides before attaching them to the bottom of the hull. The same things holds true for the deck when you get to it.

Fold the stern end of one side over along the dotted line in Illus. 90. Fold all those little tabs at the bottom over as well.

Take the bottom of the hull and place it down so that it is sitting on all those little folded tabs. Tape or glue the folded stern end to the tug's stern.

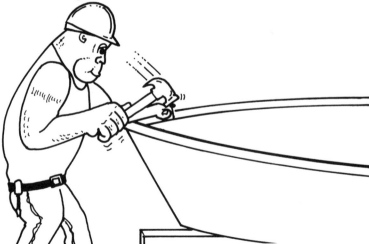

Pick up the hull and begin gluing or taping those little tabs to the underside of the hull's bottom. Keep the side tight against the hull's bottom as you work. Begin at the stern and work towards the bow of the tug. If the bow end of the side sticks out a bit past the bow of the tug, don't worry—it is supposed to. Your tug should look pretty much like the one in Illus. 91 at this point.

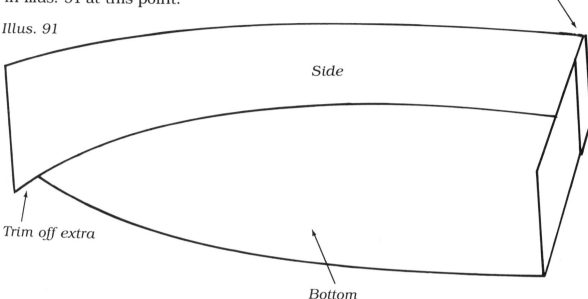

Illus. 91

Stern stands up

Side

Trim off extra

Bottom

Trim off the extra material at the bow so that the side ends at the point of the bow.

Attach the second side just as you did the first, only when you get to the bow, fold the extra material over the first side and glue or tape it down firmly. If there is more than ½-inch of material to fold over, cut off the extra so you only have ½-inch of overlap.

Now go back to the deck. Cut it out if you haven't already done so; then fold the seven tabs upwards.

If you want to make a hatch which opens, cut it in the deck towards the stern; otherwise, draw or paint a hatch on the deck.

CONSTRUCTION ZONE

Wheel House. All tugs need a wheel house from which the boat's captain controls his vessel. It usually sits atop the deck.

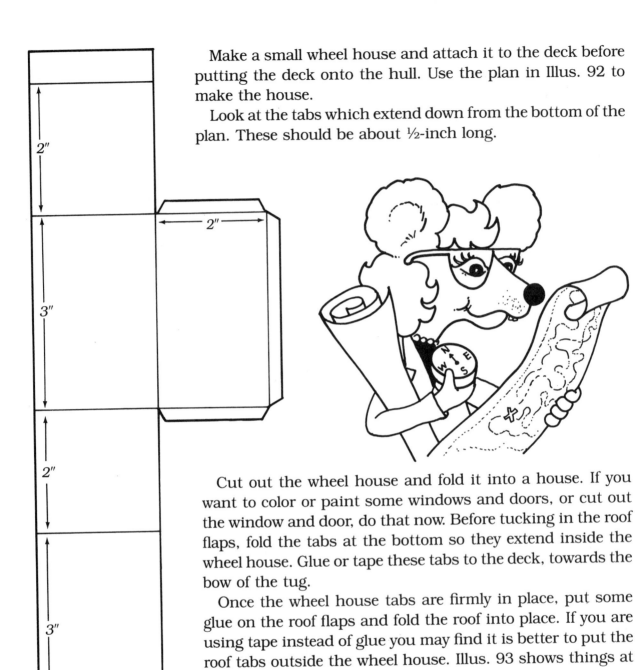

Make a small wheel house and attach it to the deck before putting the deck onto the hull. Use the plan in Illus. 92 to make the house.

Look at the tabs which extend down from the bottom of the plan. These should be about ½-inch long.

Cut out the wheel house and fold it into a house. If you want to color or paint some windows and doors, or cut out the window and door, do that now. Before tucking in the roof flaps, fold the tabs at the bottom so they extend inside the wheel house. Glue or tape these tabs to the deck, towards the bow of the tug.

Once the wheel house tabs are firmly in place, put some glue on the roof flaps and fold the roof into place. If you are using tape instead of glue you may find it is better to put the roof tabs outside the wheel house. Illus. 93 shows things at this point.

Now slip the deck inside the hull just far enough so the ends of the seven tabs reach the tops of the stern and sides. The deck will run slightly uphill towards the bow, but this is just fine as it will look like the tug's stern is low in the water as it pulls its string of barges.

Glue or tape the seven tabs to the sides and stern and your tug is ready to use. If you find the deck is a tiny bit too wide to fit into the sides, trim it with scissors. Don't trim too much or the sides won't fit tightly against the deck.

Illus. 92

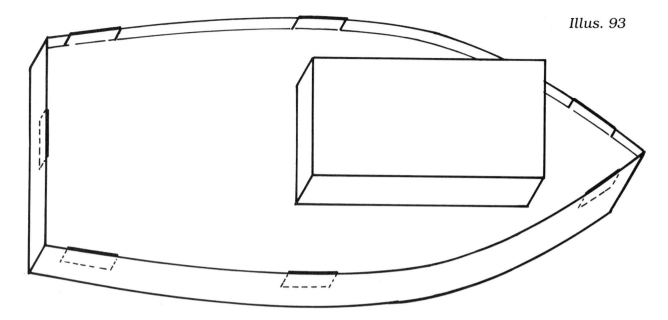

Other Vessels

You can construct oil tankers, passenger liners, or fishing trawlers the same way you made the tug. The main difference is in the shape of the hull.

An oil tanker or cargo carrier is likely to be high at both the bow and stern, as in Illus. 94, but a passenger liner will have several decks above the main deck and look like Illus. 95.

Illus. 94

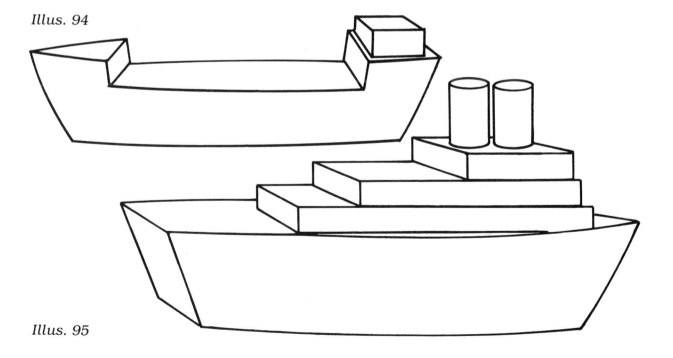

Illus. 95

Make the decks of the liner with the same sort of construction as the tug's wheel house. Make them low, long, and wide, and make each deck layer a bit smaller than the one below. Attach one layer to the top of the other just as the wheel house was attached to the tug's deck.

Round cardboard tubes make good funnels. Just cut away part of the bottom and fold back what remains as mounting tabs. Illus. 96 shows how to do this.

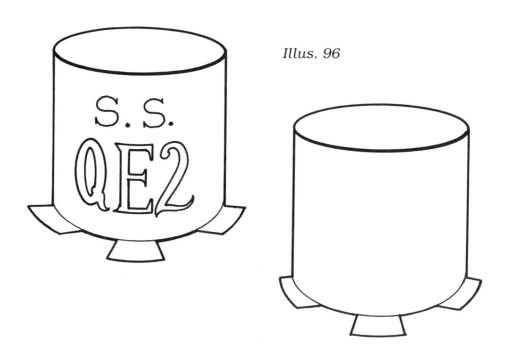

Illus. 96

74

To build a sailing vessel make the hull narrower at the stern than the tug. Illus. 97 shows a top view for such a hull. To make a mast, roll a sheet of paper tightly and tape or glue the loose end. Mount the mast by making a hole in the deck before you attach the deck to the hull. Push the mast through the deck about 1 inch. Use strips of tape to fasten it securely to the bottom of the deck. Once this is done, slip the deck into the hull.

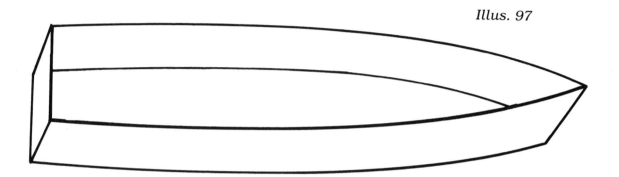

Illus. 97

Cut a triangular sail from white paper. Attach it to the mast with a bit of glue or tape at the top and bottom as in Illus. 98. Put a little bend in the sail before fastening the bottom to make it look filled by the wind.

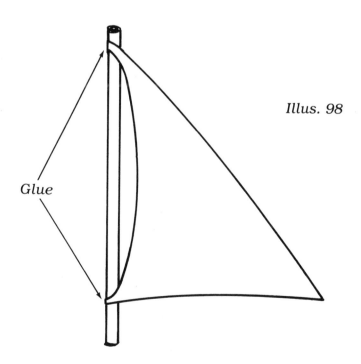

Illus. 98

Glue

Illus. 99 shows two sails mounted to one mast. Just remember that since the wind is filling the sails they are mounted at an angle and do not stick straight aft towards the stern or forward towards the bow.

Illus. 99

Not "bow," "bow!"

If you want to build a larger sailing vessel with two or even three masts you may want to use the sort of sails in Illus. 100.

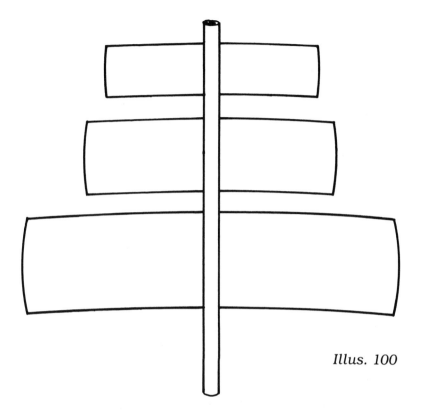

Illus. 100

How large or how small the boats and ships are depends upon you and the material you have available. Glue or tape pieces of material together to make a larger sheet of paper or cardboard.

· 4 ·
Castles
and
Forts

Medieval Castles

You probably have a pretty good idea of what a good castle looks like—a huge stone wall surrounded by a moat.

This is true of many castles but not all. Many castles did not have moats around them at all. Some were built on hilltops and depended upon the steep hillsides to slow down attackers.

Most large castles also had more than just the outer wall for protection. They had a very strong inside structure called a keep, which was the last line of defense if invaders got beyond the outer wall. Actually the castle's keep was a smaller version of the castle. It had a strong wall and usually contained the living quarters for the castle's owners.

To make a castle that can withstand an attack, begin by constructing the outer wall.

Very few castles were built as perfect squares or rectangles. Most outer walls followed the shape of the land where the castle stood. Some outer walls were quite close to the castle's keep while others were 50 or 100 yards or even more from the keep.

Some outer walls had towers. They were often round, hollow and large enough to contain one room for each floor of the tower. The towers were placed at each corner in the outer wall. They stuck out a bit past the walls so defenders had a clear view of the wall and could watch for attackers approaching the walls.

I don't think you'll need that!

Illus. 101 shows an aerial view of such a castle.

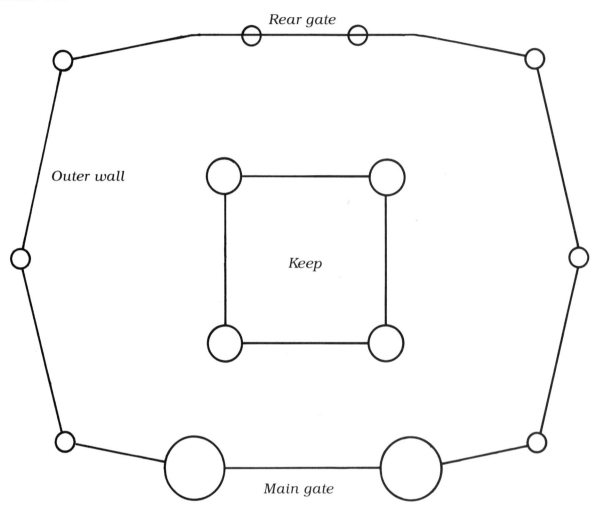

Illus. 101

Rear gate

Outer wall

Keep

Main gate

CONSTRUCTION ZONE

Battlements. Castles have a series of notches along the top. These are called battlements and are provided so defenders can shoot arrows or throw things at attackers without having to show their entire bodies and risk getting hit by an arrow.

Castle building requires fairly stiff material for walls. Cereal box cardboard is fine, so is cardboard from supermarket boxes, except that it is hard to cut.

Start with one section of the outer wall; then make as many pieces of outer wall as you want. Make the section as tall as you want, but remember the outer wall is fairly long and not as high as the keep.

Cutting battlements in the outer wall is not difficult. Cut down into the top of the material ½ inch, as in Illus. 102, then move along 1 inch and make a second cut. Fold down the section of material between the two cuts along the dotted line in Illus. 102. Cut along the fold and just like that you have a battlement. Work your way across the top of the material and your outer (or curtain) wall section will look like Illus. 103. Notice there are also cuts at either end of the section of wall. These are to fasten the wall into the tower.

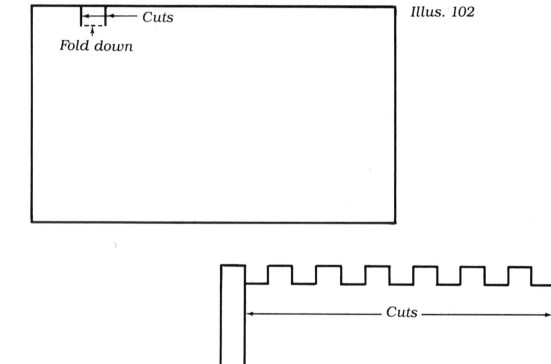

Illus. 102

Illus. 103

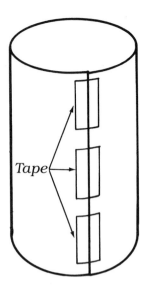

Tape

Illus. 104

To build a tower, a supply of oat cartons or gift wrapping tubes would help. If you don't have a supply of circular cartons and tubes, just roll a piece of cereal box material into a round tube as in Illus. 104. Use plenty of tape or glue to hold it together. If you use tape be sure to tape it both inside and out so the seam won't pull apart. If you use an oatmeal carton remove the top and bottom.

Illus. 105 shows how to cut slits in the tube to enable you to fasten the wall sections together. Measure the distance from the bottom of the wall to the bottom of the slit and mark that same distance up from the bottom of the tower.

Make one slit now and check to see that the section of wall fits correctly. Decide what angle the next section of wall will make; then make the second slit. Hold a piece of cardboard next to the tower at the angle. Illus. 106 shows how this works.

Illus. 105

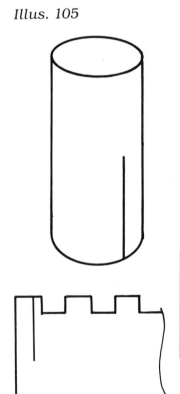

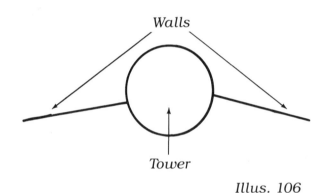

Walls

Tower

Illus. 106

Put some battlements into the top of the tower in exactly the same way you did them for the wall.

CONSTRUCTION ZONE

Turret. Towers along the outer or curtain wall are called turrets.

Don't be afraid to make square turrets. Just fold a piece of material along the four dotted lines as in Illus. 107, and tape or glue the flap firmly.

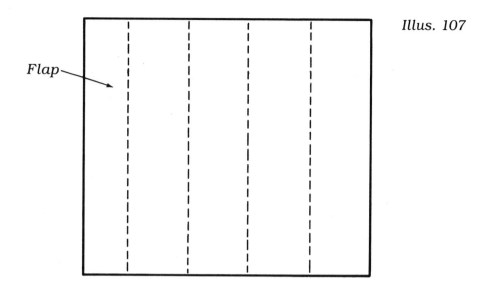

Flap

Illus. 107

Most castles had at least two gates in their outer walls, and a few had only one. Do the main gate first; then if you want a rear gate, make it in the same way, only a bit smaller.

Illus. 108 shows a front view of a castle's main gate with towers on either side of the gate. These towers are larger than the others along the curtain wall because they defend the gate.

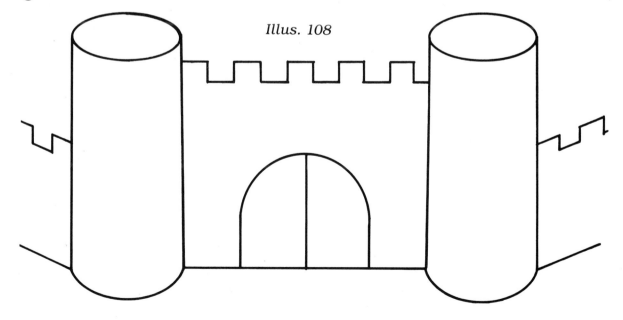

Illus. 108

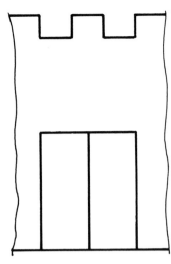

Illus. 109

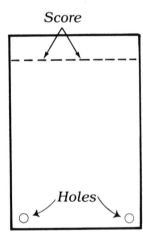

Score

Holes

Illus. 110

Notice the wall above the gate is quite a bit taller than the rest of the outer wall. This is because the wall had to be big enough to hold the gate and to let people walk above the gate on the inside walkway.

Make the gates straight across the top or arched. Illus. 109 shows the cuts in the wall between the gate towers. Cut along the dotted lines; then fold the gates open.

If the castle had a drawbridge it protected the main gate. It dropped to allow people to cross the moat and was raised as protection. Illus. 110 shows how to make a simple draw-bridge. Poke a hole in each front corner of the drawbridge; then score the dotted lines.

If you use light cardboard such as the side of a cereal box, it helps to make the folds if you score the fold first. Scoring simply means putting a little crease in the material before folding. This makes the fold nice and straight without any little crinkles in it. To score a fold use a dull table knife. Hold the dull blade close to the point, and press down hard enough to make a little groove in the material. Don't try to cut it. Just work at making a little groove. It helps to use a ruler or other straight edge to guide the knife blade. Bend the material back and forth a few times to make the fold limber enough so you can lift and lower your drawbridge. Slip the flap under the castle wall and use a couple of pieces of tape to hold it in place.

Poke a pair of holes in the front of the castle wall as in Illus. 111. Cut two pieces of string or thread long enough to reach from the front of the drawbridge up through the holes in the

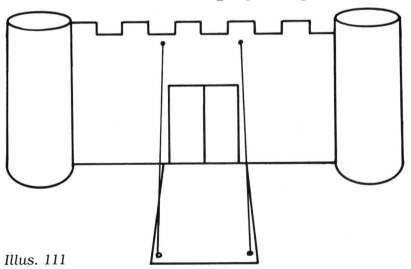

Illus. 111

castle's wall, and back to tie together behind the wall. Tie knots at the end of both pieces; then run them through the holes. Tie knots in the other end to keep the string from running back through the holes.

To raise the drawbridge just pull on the string. Make sure to leave enough string at the end to pull the bridge up. When lowering it you may need to push down on the end of the drawbridge if the fold is not limber enough.

If your castle is going to have a rear gate make it just like the main gate, except smaller.

Actual castles had defenders that walked along the top of the wall next to the battlements on a walkway. Putting a walkway around the walls isn't all that difficult to do. There are two ways to construct these walks.

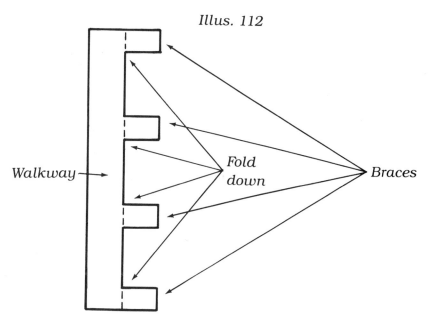

Illus. 112

Illus. 112 shows how to cut a piece of material from which to make a walkway. Cut it as wide as you wish your walkway and long enough to reach the length of the wall between towers (if necessary, make the walk into two pieces).

Fold the braces down along the dotted lines; then glue or tape them over to the inside of the outer wall.

Another way to construct walkways is shown in Illus. 113. These may be made of paper or cardboard. Cut a strip of material long enough to reach from one tower to the next, or, make the walkway in two sections.

Illus. 113

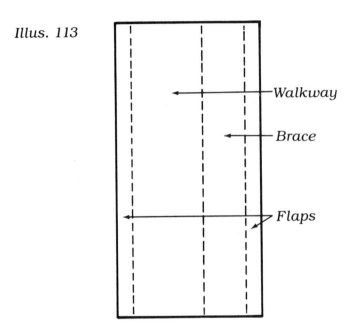

After folding the walkway along the dotted lines, tape or glue it to the inside of the wall as in Illus. 114. It's as simple as that.

Illus. 114

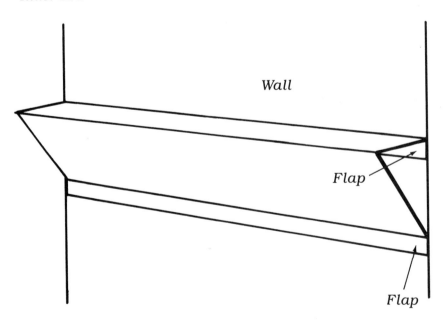

If you want, paint or color your castle to show the stones used in its building. If you make towers and turrets out of flat material, it may be easier to paint or color them before constructing the finished tower.

Since these towers and walls are part of the defensive system, it is necessary to be able to look out to watch for the enemy, and, once attackers are sighted, it is necessary to be able to fire arrows at them.

For this reason there need to be windows and arrow slits in the outer walls of the towers. Keep them narrow so enemy arrows won't come in through the openings (it will also keep the people inside the towers warm). Cut or paint windows and arrow slits in your towers and along the walls themselves. Illus. 115 shows a few designs for archery slits.

Illus. 115

With the outer wall complete, it is time to build the castle's keep. Since you already know how to construct walls and towers you don't need to worry about these items. Just keep in mind that the keep will have larger towers and higher walls than the outer wall. Also, most keeps are built either as squares or rectangles.

The keep is square because it was easier to defend a four-sided keep than one with more sides. While the outer wall follows the humps and bumps of the land, the keep, being smaller, was built on a relatively level piece of ground.

Give the keep a main gate. Many old castles in Europe have towers on either side of the keep's main gate. If you decide to give your castle's keep a pair of gate towers, they should look very much like those on the outer wall.

Illus. 116 shows the inside of a keep's wall with two walkways in place. Since the keep is fairly tall it may have two or three or even four stories. Remember to line up the arrow slits so archers standing on a walkway can use them.

Illus. 116

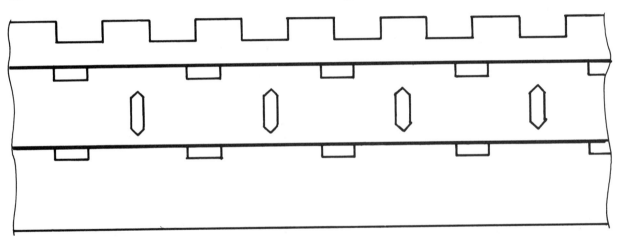

A castle consisted of more than just walls and towers. There were many small stone or even wooden buildings between the outer walls and the keep. These were used for storage, as stables for the knights' horses, and for shops for those who served the king and his knights, such as carpenters and blacksmiths.

Check with Chapter One for the plans of village buildings. Make the doors and windows smaller than you would for modern buildings. To make a stable or any open shed, first construct a building; then cut away most of one wall. Just like that you have a stable or shed.

There's even a job for you!

Most of the great castles contained a chapel. If you decide to build a chapel, it can have a steep roof, it can be long and narrow, but it won't have a steeple. The chapel should be close to or even inside the keep.

One final touch to your castle is overhanging parapets or turrets along the outer wall. Illus. 117 shows how such a structure might look.

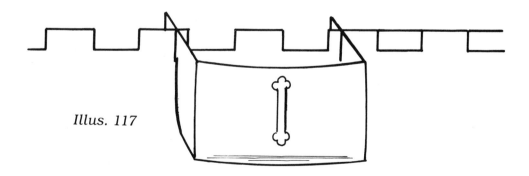

Illus. 117

To make a few of these parapets, begin with a piece of material 8 × 4 inches as in Illus. 118. Construct your parapet from stiff paper or light cardboard, or make the first one from notebook paper, which is easy to cut and fold.

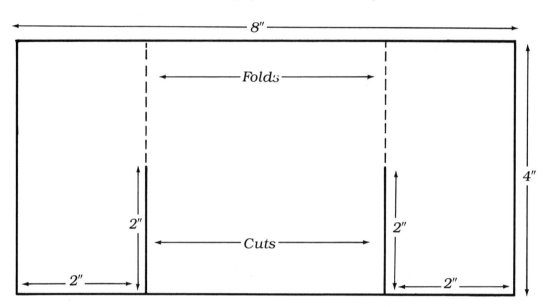

Make the two cuts shown by the arrows in Illus. 119. These should be 2 inches from either side. Each cut is 2 inches long.

Fold the paper above the cuts. These folds are indicated by the dotted lines in the illustration.

Cut away the two sections shown by the shaded areas in Illus. 119. These areas are each about 2½ inches long and ½-inch wide. Make the two cuts shown by the arrows in the illustration. Each of these cuts needs to be about ¾-inch long. Add the three arrow slits as shown by either cutting them out or drawing them.

Illus. 119

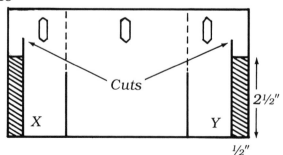

To construct the parapet, bend (don't fold) the two sections marked "X" and "Y" together so they overlap slightly. Your parapet looks like Illus. 120. Bend the center down over the two sides and it now appears as in Illus. 121.

Illus. 120

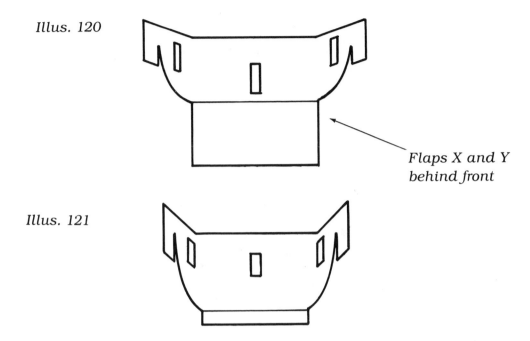

Flaps X and Y behind front

Illus. 121

Tape or glue the flaps and bottom together and you're ready to hang the parapet on the castle's wall. Trim off any corner that might stick out with scissors. It all depends on the angle after you bend the flaps and bottom into place whether anything sticks out or not.

Find the point on the castle wall where you want to put the parapet. Hold it against the wall and cut two slits in the top of the wall, each ¾-inch deep, so each slit is opposite the slits in your parapet. Illus. 122 shows how.

Illus. 122

Slits in wall

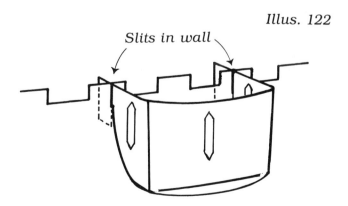

Make as many parapets as you wish and your castle is finally complete.

How large or how small you make your castle depends upon how much time you wish to spend on it and where you plan to play with it. This isn't a project you will finish in just an hour or so. The great thing, though, is since the castle is put together with interlocking walls and towers, you can add to it any time you wish.

Log Forts

Forts from the American Old West were usually pretty much square in shape and lacked a keep, which served as a final protection for defenders. Forts were built quickly and were never intended to last for hundreds of years.

The best way to assemble a fort is to make an outer wall similar to the one around the castle (pages 82–83). Illus. 123 shows the sort of outer wall for a fort. You can draw or paint in each individual log. The pointed tips may be as wide or as narrow as you want depending upon the size logs used in the fort.

Illus. 123

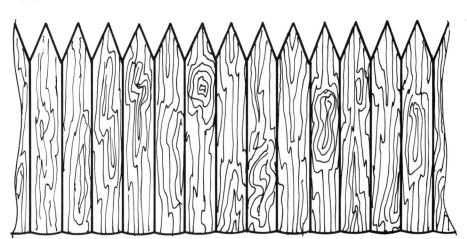

Illus. 124 gives an idea for another type of fort. This one was made of *adobe*, or bricks made of clay mixed with straw. Forts of this type were common in the southwest United States.

Illus. 124

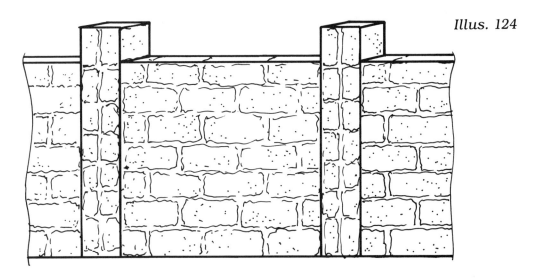

Fasten the corners of the fort together as shown in Illus. 125. It shows how to cut a slot up from the bottom of one section so it interlocks with the slot cut down from the top of the adjoining section.

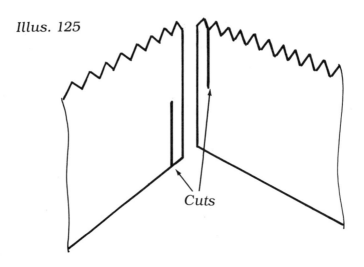

Illus. 125

Cuts

The dotted lines in Illus. 126 show where to cut so the gate will open and close.

The wall is built higher over the gate than on either side so it all won't pull apart when the gate opens.

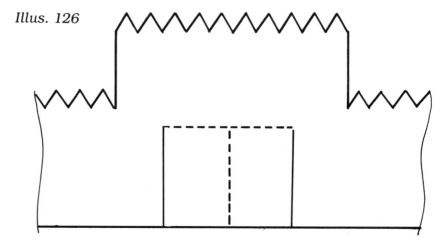

Illus. 126

A good fort had a tower, or blockhouse, at each corner. These towers or blockhouses stuck out past the walls of the fort. Building these blockhouses is pretty much the same as constructing square castle towers (page 85). Make the first blockhouse 4 inches square.

Illus. 127 shows the blockhouse plan. Keep in mind that the blockhouse is about 2 inches taller than the height of the fort's walls. The four tabs which extend up from the top of the walls will hold the roof in place. Cut a few firing windows (sometimes they were called loopholes) out before you assemble the blockhouse.

Illus. 127

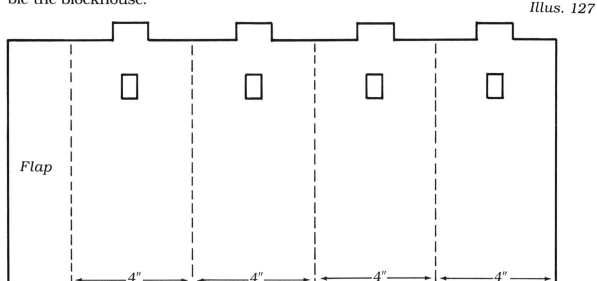

Flap

|← 4" →|← 4" →|← 4" →|← 4" →|

Fold the blockhouse along the dotted lines and glue or tape the flap inside to hold the building together. Bend the roof tabs down a bit but don't fold them since they will be sticking up slightly when the roof is attached.

A blockhouse for a blockhead.

Now fit the blockhouse into place at the corner of the fort. Cut two slots in the fort as in Illus. 128. These should be an inch or so from the corner. Hold the blockhouse above the corner and cut a pair of slots in two blockhouse walls, as in Illus. 129. Since the blockhouse is taller than the fort's walls, cut them about half the height of the fort's walls; then check the cuts by slipping the blockhouse onto the walls. If the blockhouse does not quite reach the ground, just lengthen the slots a bit.

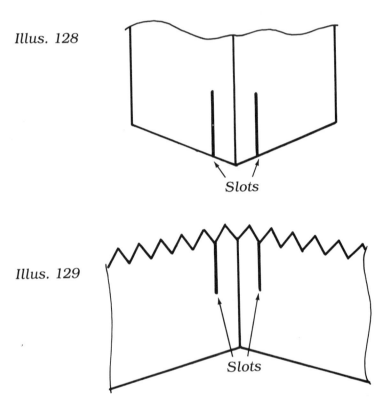

Illus. 128

Slots

Illus. 129

Slots

To put a roof on the blockhouse, draw the plan seen in Illus. 130. If you make larger or smaller blockhouses than this one, remember to adjust the roof's dimensions.

Here's a time-saving hint. Since you are going to make four of these roof sections, cut out the section and draw around it three more times for the other roof pieces (if you are using paper, you could hold three sheets of paper under the pattern and cut all four at once). Another idea is to fold a sheet of notebook or typing paper into fourths; then draw the plan on the top layer and cut out all four pieces at once. Cutting the pieces apart along the folds is better than drawing four plans.

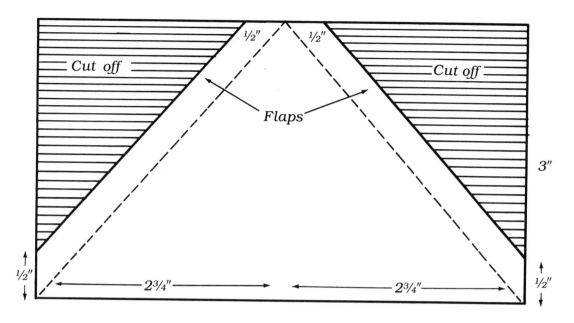

Fold down the flaps so each roof section looks like Illus. 131. Glue the flap of one section to that of another as in Illus. 132. Add sections three and four, pulling into a point the last tab of section four and the tab of section one. If you use tape rather than glue, just fasten the four sections together by taping the tabs; then, when the roof is pulled together, run a strip of tape along the top of the roof at each point two sections come together.

Illus. 131

Illus. 132

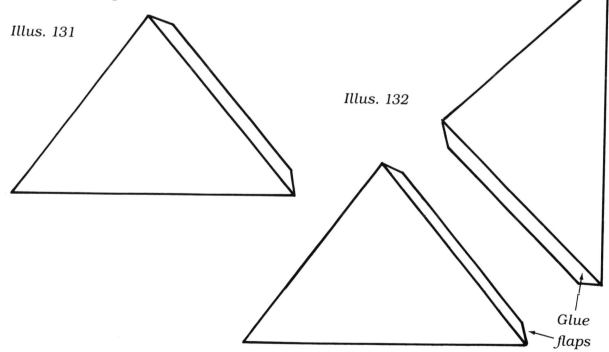

Glue
flaps

To set the roof on top of the blockhouse, glue or tape the four tabs on the blockhouse walls to the underside of the roof.

Most good forts had a watchtower. The watchtower was tall enough to give soldiers a view of the surrounding country-side. Sometimes this watchtower was located in the middle of the fort; in other forts one blockhouse was taller than the others and it became the watchtower.

To build a watchtower use exactly the same approach used in making the corner blockhouses, except make it much taller. Everything else, including making and attaching the roof, is just the same as for a blockhouse. When the watch-tower is completed, use it instead of a blockhouse at one corner of the fort, or to be a little fancier, place it near the middle of the fort. Cut out two sections on each side of the tower, as in Illus. 133, to give the tower the look of having been built of poles and beams (which is the way many watch-towers were actually constructed). Just don't cut away so much material that the tower is unsteady and, above all, don't poke or cut yourself when you begin cutting.

Illus. 133

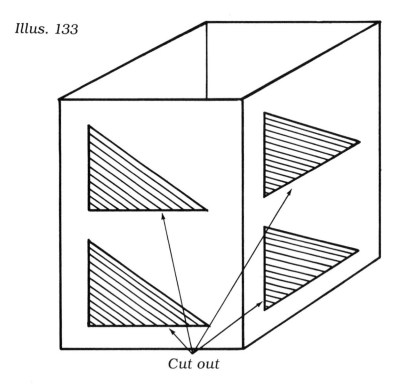

Cut out

The fort needs walkways for soldiers along the walls, since they are taller than the men and women inside. Walls inside a fort are often called catwalks.

Locate the catwalks so soldiers and others inside the fort can stand on them and be able to fire over the top of the wall between the pointed ends of the logs. Build them the same as the castle's walkways (pages 87–89).

Here's another idea. Instead of having defenders fire over the top of the fort, cut loopholes in the wall every so often. Illus. 134 shows how these loopholes may look in a section of the fort's wall.

Illus. 134

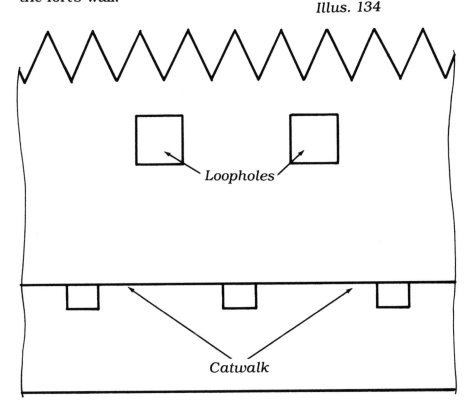

Loopholes

Catwalk

Forts served as the living quarters for many people. Not only did soldiers live in them, but also merchants, craftsmen, guides, and others made their homes there. These people needed houses and shops inside the fort's walls. Horses were also stabled inside the forts.

You can make the buildings the same way you did with the Pre-Fab (page 14), and you can cut one side from a building to turn it into a stable or a shop with an open front. You can also use a few different building styles.

Illus. 135 shows how to make the walls for a log cabin. Notice that the logs are exactly ½-inch wide and so is the space between each pair of logs. This is very important since the logs from one side of the cabin will interlock with the logs from another side. The logs at one end of a cabin will stick out at the bottom and end with a space at the top, and at the opposite end of that wall the logs stick out at the top and have a space at the wall's bottom. This is so one wall will interlock with another wall perfectly.

Illus. 135

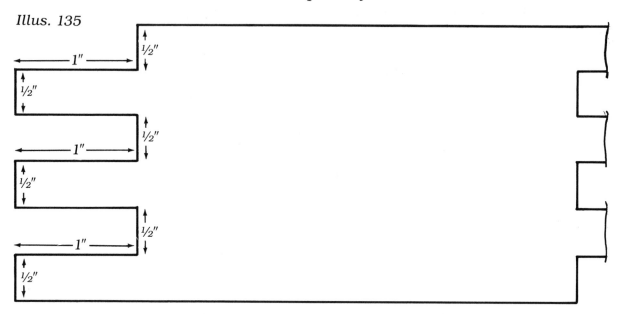

Build the log walls as high as you wish. Those in Illus. 135 are only 6 logs high (3 inches if each log is exactly ½ inch side). Make the cabin walls as long as you wish, and any shape you wish. The cabin may have two walls one length and two walls a bit longer or shorter.

Illus. 136

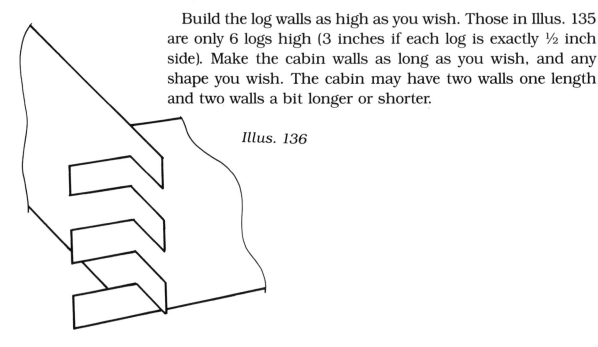

Cut a door in one end of the cabin and a window or two in the other walls; then assemble your log cabin by interlocking the walls as in Illus. 136. Use a couple of pieces of cellophane tape inside the walls to hold them firmly together at the corners.

There are two types of roofs you can make. If the cabin is square, you can make the same roof as you used for your blockhouses by adding a tab at the top of each log wall to fasten the roof into place. Illus. 137 shows a log wall with the roof tab at the top.

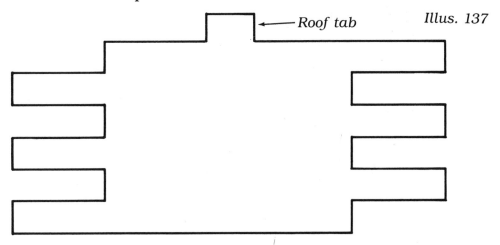

← *Roof tab*   *Illus. 137*

You're no Lone Ranger!

If you built a rectangular cabin, give it a peaked roof. Illus. 138 shows how to plan the ends of the peaked roof for a 4-inch-square cabin. Make two of these exactly alike, one for the front and one for the rear of the cabin.

Illus. 138

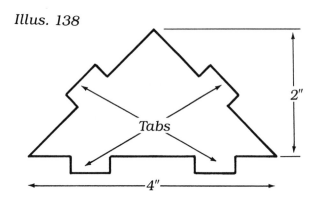

Illus. 139

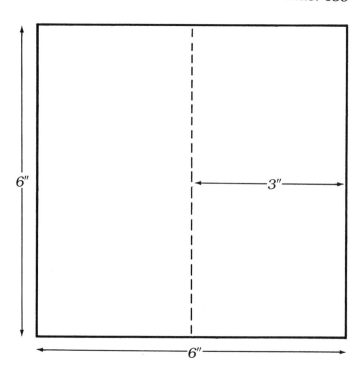

Illus. 139 shows the roof itself. It will fit a cabin 4 inches wide and 5 inches long and have a bit of overhang. If your cabin is larger or smaller, adjust the measurements for your roof. The dotted line shows where to fold the roof.

To attach the roof to your log cabin, glue or tape the bottom flaps on the ends to the inside of the front and rear cabin walls; then fold the top flaps down and glue or tape the roof in place. That's all there is to it.

To add a little more variety to the buildings, make a building with a flat, sloping roof (builders call this a shed roof). This sort of building makes a great stable or blacksmith shop.

The plan in Illus. 140 is for a shed-type building 4 × 5 inches and 4 inches tall on the high side. Notice the way the sides are positioned so when you fold the building together the 4-inch-wide sides will be opposite each other as will the sides which are 5 inches wide.

Study the way the sloping sides are drawn. The tabs which stick up from all four sides are used to fasten the roof into place. Cut away the shaded area.

Illus. 140

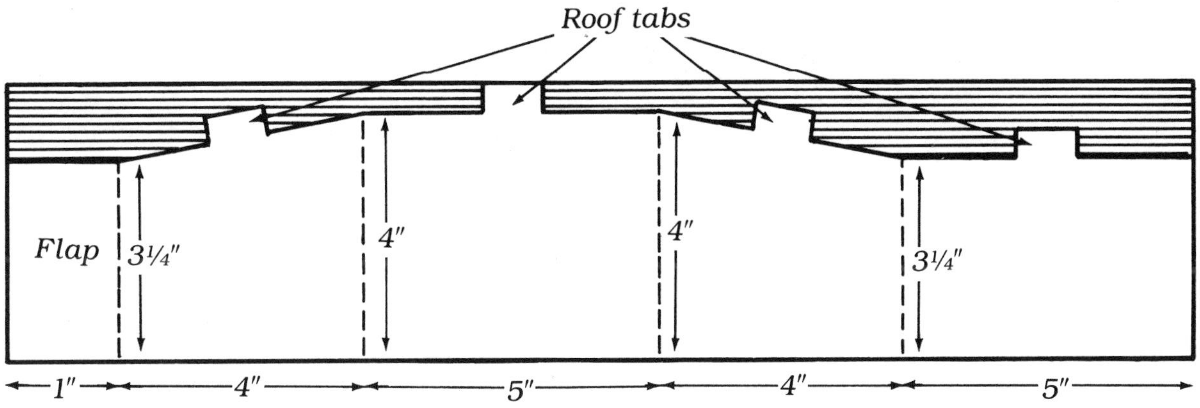

Roof tabs

Flap   3¼"   4"   4"   3¼"

←1"→ ←—4"—→ ←——5"——→ ←——4"——→ ←——5"——→

Cut out the building and fold it into a four-sided structure, then tape or glue the flap on the inside of the shed to hold it together. Fold the roof tabs down and the shed looks pretty much like Illus. 141.

Illus. 141

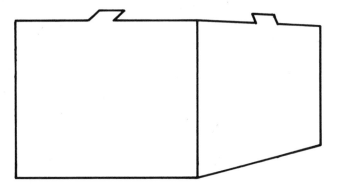

Cut a flat piece of material just a little longer than the sloping side of your shed and just a bit wider than the shed. This will give your roof an overhang. Glue or tape the tabs and press the roof into place, and the shed is finished.

Cut away some of the high side of the shed (the shaded area in Illus. 142) to open it up for use as a stable or shop. Or, just cut a door and maybe a window or two into the shed.

Illus. 142

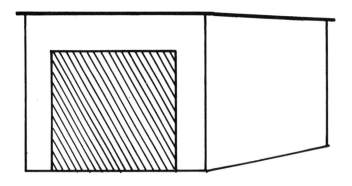

Make the fort and its buildings as large or as small as you wish. Don't try to make all the inside buildings at once. Build the fort and play with it; then the next time you want to play with it, put it together in a minute or two and build a few inside buildings. If you add a few buildings at a time you can use the fort and watch it grow without spending too many hours getting it all put together.

And you're no Tonto!

· 5 ·
Stadium

Since early Roman and Greek times, people have enjoyed going to sports stadiums. With a cardboard box, some stiff paper or cereal box material and a little inventiveness, you can make a sports stadium of your own—one that you can simply build for the fun of it to use with miniature figures or even model race cars.

There is no limit as to the size of your stadium except for the size of the available material. You can make a stadium from a shoe box and the lid can become the dome in case of bad weather. You can make a stadium large enough to fill one of the large cardboard boxes from the supermarket.

Since the size of your stadium is entirely up to you, the directions and suggestions which follow won't include a lot of dimensions. Just carefully measure the size of the box you are starting with and you will be fine.

Decide first of all how you want to use your stadium. Will it be a combination baseball-football-track-event center, or will you be using it for auto racing? This makes a difference in how large the open area in the center will be and how much room is left for seating.

Once you have decided how much open area you need for the playing field, track, and the like, you know how much seating your stadium can have.

For the first stadium seating use stiff typing or notebook paper. This is better than cereal box material for beginning work.

Fold the sheet into a fan fold (a strip up; then back) with each fold about ⅝-inch wide. Fold one edge over as in Illus. 143. Turn the page over and fold it again so that the second fold is exactly the same width as the first. Turn the paper over again and fold once more. Illus. 144 shows the paper after several folds.

Keep on turning and folding until the entire sheet of paper has become ⅝-inch wide and many layers thick.

When you open the paper it looks like a series of hills and valleys.

To turn the fan-folded paper into stadium seating, tape or glue the bottom edge to the stadium floor. Open the rest of the paper into a series of right angles and fasten the top edge to the stadium wall. Illus. 145 shows a side view of this step.

If one sheet of paper isn't long enough to reach from the edge of the playing field or track to the stadium wall, just fold another sheet of paper or two into fans. Glue or tape the sheets together by overlapping one fold on the first sheet with a fold on the second. There is no limit as to how far you can make the seating reach by splicing sheets of folded paper together.

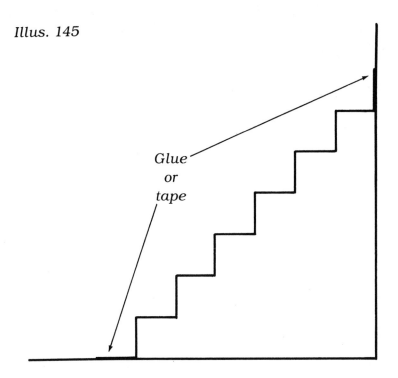

Glue
or
tape

By now you have probably discovered a problem. The seating seems to want to fold down instead of staying upright. To solve the problem, cut a rectangle of cereal box material about ¾ inch longer and higher than the dotted rectangle in Illus. 146.

Illus. 146

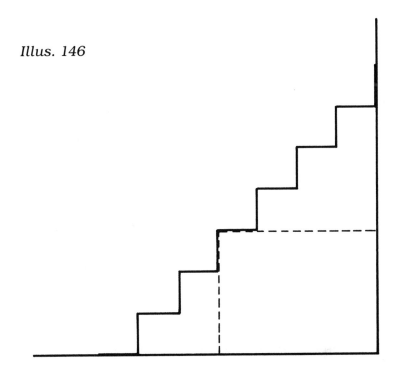

The shaded area in Illus. 147 shows how to cut out two corners of this rectangle. After removing the corners, fold the three sides along the dotted lines. This is a brace to hold the seating in place.

Illus. 147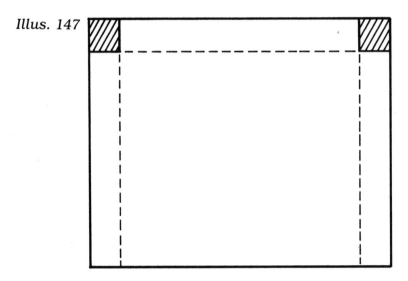

Slip the brace beneath the seating so one fold is on the top and the other folds are to the right and left. Illus. 148 shows the brace in place.

Illus. 148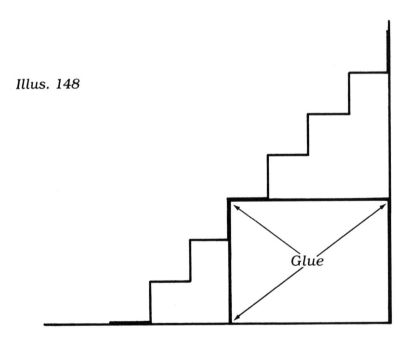

Glue or tape the rear of the brace to the stadium wall. Attach the back and bottom of one row of seats to the top and other side of the brace, and the seating is lots more solid than it was. Depending on how high and long the seats are, put in several braces to hold each section of seating.

Splicing the end of one paper to the end of another will also make a section stronger. However, splice the paper before folding. No matter how careful you are, it is almost impossible to fold two sheets of paper exactly the same with fan folds.

Install braces of different sizes to support many rows of seats. Illus. 149 shows a low, wide brace in place with a taller brace behind it.

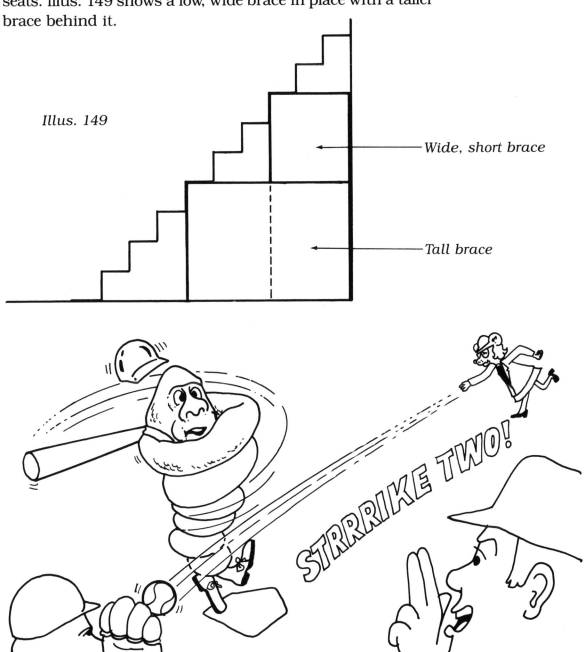

Illus. 149

Wide, short brace

Tall brace

STRRRIKE TWO!

Corners can be a problem to fill with seats. Illus. 150 shows a top view of such a corner. The trick is to cut two pieces of fan-folded material at an angle. In order to make the two sections fit together properly, cut out a little triangle of material from every other row on one of the sections of seating. Illus. 151 shows these cuts (the shaded areas). If you cut the two corner sections from the same sheet of folded paper, the folds will be the same and the two sections will fit together.

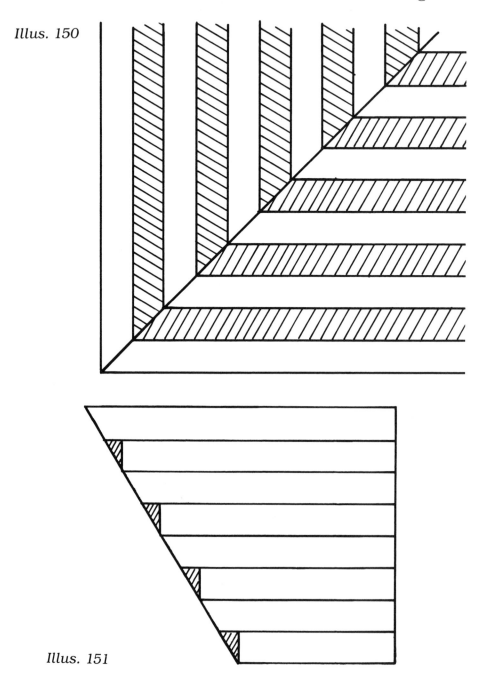

Illus. 150

Illus. 151

All a round or oval stadium takes is a bit of planning and some extra cutting and fitting. Use the same method as the corners to form seating around an oval end of the stadium.

Make a circular stadium in the same manner. Cut the sections of seating at a different angle than for the corner. Use the section of fan-folded paper you cut out to make the two corner pieces for a rectangular stadium. Illus. 152 shows this. The center section, marked with an "X," is overlapped by the two side sections in forming a curve. Cut the ends and overlap the next section (and so on) to complete the curve.

Illus. 152

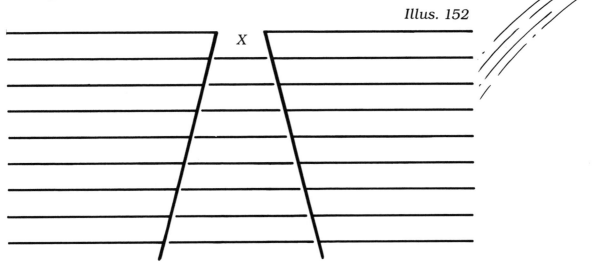

Since it takes so much cutting and fitting to build a circular stadium, it's best to make your first one rectangular and only worry about fitting a few corners.

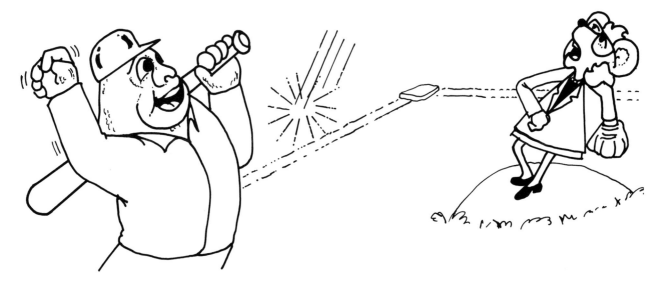

Every stadium needs a scoreboard. The best place to put the scoreboard is at one end of the stadium. It can be either an end without seating or one in which the seating ends beneath the scoreboard. Illus. 153 shows a couple of ideas.

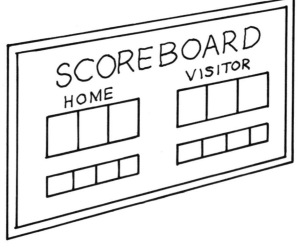

Illus. 153

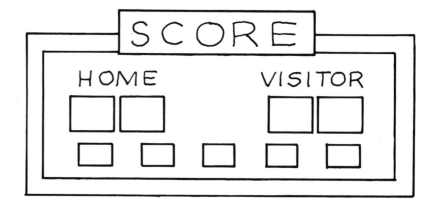

Make two tunnels between rows of seating for players or drivers to enter the stadium. Illus. 154 shows one way such tunnels look from the playing field.

Illus. 154

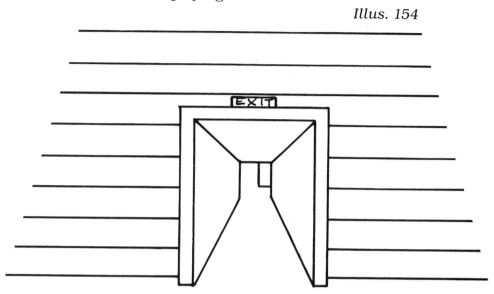

Fans need to get in and out of the stadium, so remember to paint some entrances on the outside of the stadium. Illus. 155 shows how to cut simple entrances which open and close. If you wish (and have a steady hand) make the entrances a bit fancier by arching their tops. Just don't cut your hand or the furniture.

Illus. 155

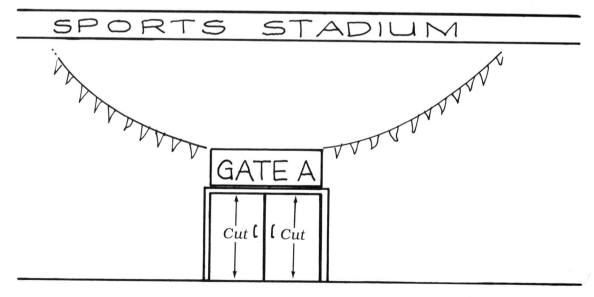

Putting a dome on a circular stadium isn't difficult. Illus. 156 shows how to cut out a small section from a round piece of material. Pull side "Z" over to side "Y" and tape or glue the sides together. This forms a flattened cone which will make a perfect dome. The center of the cone can be made higher with a larger section of material.

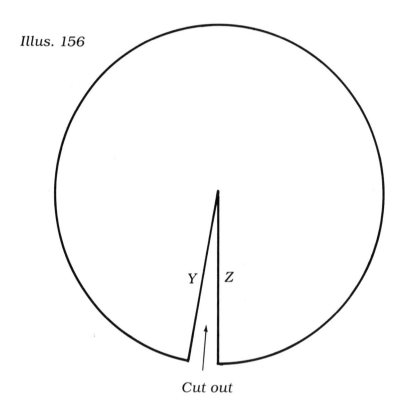

Illus. 156

Cut out

The great thing about a stadium is that you can add to it after playing with it for a time. You don't have to put in all the detail before you begin using it. If you get bored with the scoreboard, change it. Or, try cutting out different types of fields with construction paper so you can easily change games. Illus. 157 shows an example.

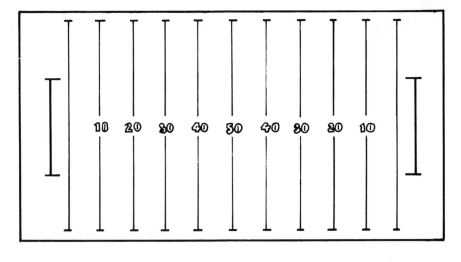

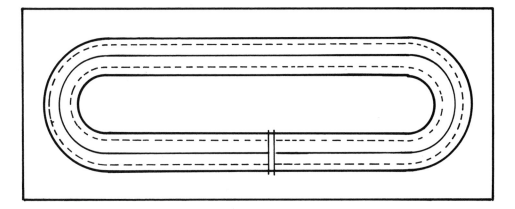

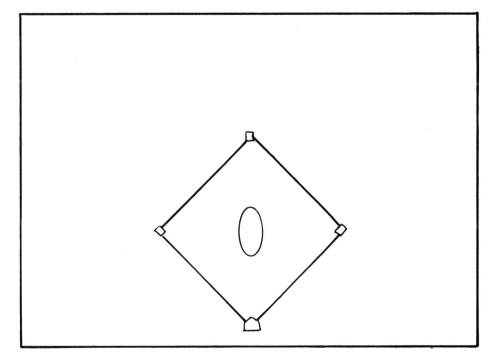

METRIC EQUIVALENCY CHART

MM—MILLIMETRES   CM—CENTIMETRES

INCHES TO MILLIMETRES AND CENTIMETRES

INCHES	MM	CM	INCHES	CM	INCHES	CM
1/8	3	0.3	9	22.9	30	76.2
1/4	6	0.6	10	25.4	31	78.7
3/8	10	1.0	11	27.9	32	81.3
1/2	13	1.3	12	30.5	33	83.8
5/8	16	1.6	13	33.0	34	86.4
3/4	19	1.9	14	35.6	35	88.9
7/8	22	2.2	15	38.1	36	91.4
1	25	2.5	16	40.6	37	94.0
1 1/4	32	3.2	17	43.2	38	96.5
1 1/2	38	3.8	18	45.7	39	99.1
1 3/4	44	4.4	19	48.3	40	101.6
2	51	5.1	20	50.8	41	104.1
2 1/2	64	6.4	21	53.3	42	106.7
3	76	7.6	22	55.9	43	109.2
3 1/2	89	8.9	23	58.4	44	111.8
4	102	10.2	24	61.0	45	114.3
4 1/2	114	11.4	25	63.5	46	116.8
5	127	12.7	26	66.0	47	119.4
6	152	15.2	27	68.6	48	121.9
7	178	17.8	28	71.1	49	124.5
8	203	20.3	29	73.7	50	127.0

YARDS TO METRES

YARDS	METRES	YARDS	METRES	YARDS	METRES	YARDS	METRES	YARDS	METRES
1/8	0.11	2 1/8	1.94	4 1/8	3.77	6 1/8	5.60	8 1/8	7.43
1/4	0.23	2 1/4	2.06	4 1/4	3.89	6 1/4	5.72	8 1/4	7.54
3/8	0.34	2 3/8	2.17	4 3/8	4.00	6 3/8	5.83	8 3/8	7.66
1/2	0.46	2 1/2	2.29	4 1/2	4.11	6 1/2	5.94	8 1/2	7.77
5/8	0.57	2 5/8	2.40	4 5/8	4.23	6 5/8	6.06	8 5/8	7.89
3/4	0.69	2 3/4	2.51	4 3/4	4.34	6 3/4	6.17	8 3/4	8.00
7/8	0.80	2 7/8	2.63	4 7/8	4.46	6 7/8	6.29	8 7/8	8.12
1	0.91	3	2.74	5	4.57	7	6.40	9	8.23
1 1/8	1.03	3 1/8	2.86	5 1/8	4.69	7 1/8	6.52	9 1/8	8.34
1 1/4	1.14	3 1/4	2.97	5 1/4	4.80	7 1/4	6.63	9 1/4	8.46
1 3/8	1.26	3 3/8	3.09	5 3/8	4.91	7 3/8	6.74	9 3/8	8.57
1 1/2	1.37	3 1/2	3.20	5 1/2	5.03	7 1/2	6.86	9 1/2	8.69
1 5/8	1.49	3 5/8	3.31	5 5/8	5.14	7 5/8	6.97	9 5/8	8.80
1 3/4	1.60	3 3/4	3.43	5 3/4	5.26	7 3/4	7.09	9 3/4	8.92
1 7/8	1.71	3 7/8	3.54	5 7/8	5.37	7 7/8	7.20	9 7/8	9.03
2	1.83	4	3.66	6	5.49	8	7.32	10	9.14

INDEX